Susan Sontag

Titles in the series Critical Lives present the work of leading cultural figures of the modern period. Each book explores the life of the artist, writer, philosopher or architect in question and relates it to their major works.

In the same series

Georges Bataille *Stuart Kendall* • Charles Baudelaire *Rosemary Lloyd* • Simone de Beauvoir *Ursula Tidd* • Samuel Beckett *Andrew Gibson* • Walter Benjamin *Esther Leslie* John Berger *Andy Merrifield* • Jorge Luis Borges *Jason Wilson* • Constantin Brancusi *Sanda Miller* • Bertolt Brecht *Philip Glahn* • Charles Bukowski *David Stephen Calonne* • William S. Burroughs *Phil Baker* • John Cage *Rob Haskins* • Fidel Castro *Nick Caistor* • Coco Chanel *Linda Simon* • Noam Chomsky *Wolfgang B. Sperlich* • Jean Cocteau *James S. Williams* • Salvador Dalí *Mary Ann Caws* • Guy Debord *Andy Merrifield* • Claude Debussy *David J. Code* • Fyodr Dostoevsky *Robert Bird* • Marcel Duchamp *Caroline Cros* • Sergei Eisenstein *Mike O'Mahony* • Michel Foucault *David Macey* • Mahatma Gandhi *Douglas Allen* • Jean Genet *Stephen Barber* • Allen Ginsberg *Steve Finbow* • Derek Jarman *Michael Charlesworth* • Alfred Jarry *Jill Fell* • James Joyce *Andrew Gibson* • Carl Jung *Paul Bishop* • Franz Kafka *Sander L. Gilman* • Frida Kahlo *Gannit Ankori* • Yves Klein *Nuit Banai* • Lenin *Lars T. Lih* • Stéphane Mallarmé *Roger Pearson* • Gabriel García Márquez *Stephen M. Hart* • Karl Marx *Paul Thomas* Eadweard Muybridge *Marta Braun* • Vladimir Nabokov *Barbara Wyllie* • Pablo Neruda *Dominic Moran* • Octavio Paz *Nick Caistor* • Pablo Picasso *Mary Ann Caws* Edgar Allan Poe *Kevin J. Hayes* • Ezra Pound *Alec Marsh* • Marcel Proust *Adam Watt* Jean-Paul Sartre *Andrew Leak* • Erik Satie *Mary E. Davis* • Arthur Schopenhauer *Peter B. Lewis* • Susan Sontag *Jerome Boyd Maunsell* •Gertrude Stein *Lucy Daniel* • Richard Wagner *Raymond Furness* • Simone Weil *Palle Yourgrau* • Ludwig Wittgenstein *Edward Kanterian* • Frank Lloyd Wright *Robert McCarter*

Susan Sontag

Jerome Boyd Maunsell

REAKTION BOOKS

for Tessa

Published by Reaktion Books Ltd
33 Great Sutton Street
London EC1V 0DX, UK

www.reaktionbooks.co.uk

First published 2014

Copyright © Jerome Boyd Maunsell 2014

Printed and bound in Great Britain by Bell & Bain, Glasgow

A catalogue record for this book is available from the British Library

ISBN 978 1 78023 288 1

Contents

Susan Sontag by Henri Cartier-Bresson, 1972.

1

Beginnings, 1933–1950

In the end we all return to our beginnings.
Susan Sontag, 'American Spirits' (1978)

Susan Sontag wrote essays, film scripts, novels, plays, short stories – and her essays, in particular, display an extraordinary range of interests, in art, cinema, dance, drama, politics, photography and opera, as well as literature, always her first love – but she never wrote an autobiography portraying her life in full. In the early 1970s, soon to turn 40, she thought very briefly about writing a book structured around several different themes in her life, although she never did so, perhaps because she felt it was too early.[1] In later years, especially in the 1990s, as her son David Rieff tells us, she thought of writing a memoir based not on her own life so much as her friendships. The list of figures Sontag knew and could have portrayed in this way encompasses many artistic and intellectual luminaries: Joseph Brodsky, Elizabeth Hardwick, Jasper Johns, Herbert Marcuse and Paul Thek, to name only a few.[2] This project was likewise never attempted, joining the ranks of the books Sontag planned to write one day.

But Sontag did publish two fragmentary autobiographical pieces in her lifetime: the short memoir 'Pilgrimage' and the short story 'Project for a Trip to China', which deal with aspects of her childhood, each painting it in a different light. 'Pilgrimage' turns mainly on a visit Sontag paid as a teenager to the writer

Thomas Mann at his home in Los Angeles in the late 1940s; 'Project for a Trip to China' focuses on Sontag's father and on her preparations to visit China, where she was probably conceived, for the first time. The tone in 'Pilgrimage', written in the mid-1980s and published in the *New Yorker*, is ironic, self-mocking, contemptuous, wondrous, embarrassed; while 'Project for a Trip to China', written in the 1970s, displays humour, pathos, nostalgia and melancholy. Both pieces reveal, in recounting different voyages away from herself, much about Sontag's childhood and her attitude towards it.

Privately, Sontag also kept a diary from her early adolescence onwards, which by her death ran to around a hundred notebooks. The diaries record her life as it was lived, and as she wanted to live it, day by day, with an incredible, even exemplary, avidity for books, for experience, for love, for conversation, for knowledge, for art, for company – almost a series of different, overlapping lives. As they went on, increasingly the diaries became creative workbooks as well, listing ideas for essays, stories and novels alongside accounts of Sontag's life and loves. They also contain, intermittently but persistently, fragments of reflective autobiography on Sontag's family and origins, including two lists of memories she wrote in 1957, turning 24, called 'Notes of a Childhood'. Made up of disconnected phrases, impressions and sentences, recounted in the first list without chronological order and grouped into two sections in the second, these 'Notes' are true to the workings of memory in their lack of sequence and give a raw portrait of Sontag's youth.

The brevity of these texts on youth suggests an unwillingness to look back and reminisce for long, while the repeated attempts show her fascination. Sontag also often spoke about her youth in interviews. Her childhood, she said, was a 'prison sentence' from which she escaped as soon as possible.[3] All her life she retained an uneasy sense, painful and liberating, of not fitting into her own childhood, of being alien to her beginnings. As an adult Sontag tried to extricate herself from her own early biography, yet all her fragmentary attempts, other than the diaries, to write autobiography deal only with the very beginnings which she disavowed: a childhood of half-formed allegiances, arrivals and departures, enticingly glimpsed vistas that soon faded from view forever.

Susan Rosenblatt, later Sontag, was born in Manhattan on 16 January 1933, the first child of Jack Rosenblatt and Mildred Jacobson, who were both in their mid-to-late twenties and ran a fur trading business in China. Susan's young parents had been raised in New York and came from Jewish families which had left Europe for America: Jack's parents, Samuel and Gussie, from Austria, and Mildred's parents, Isaac and Dora, from Russian-occupied Poland.[4] Much of this heritage was lost on the young Susan. In middle age, Susan recalled asking her father's mother, who died when Susan was seven, where she came from, and being told, simply, 'Europe'.[5] She asked again and received the same answer; even in the 1970s she said that she did not know exactly where the Rosenblatts came from.

Susan's parents were away in China for much of her early childhood. Mildred came back from China to Manhattan to deliver Susan, yet she returned there after the birth, leaving Susan with the extended family in New York. An Irish nanny, Rose McNulty, or 'Rosie', played a large role in bringing up Susan over the following years. Mildred revisited New York to have a second child, Judith, on 27 February 1936; Susan remembered visiting her in hospital with Rosie after the birth.[6] Mildred again departed for China, leaving the two sisters in the family home in Great Neck, Long Island, which, as Susan later wrote, was filled with things from the other, 'real' Chinese house, 'the one I never saw'.[7] Chinese ebony swinging doors gave on to the living room of the house in Great Neck, filled with 'trophies' and objects still recalled in middle age: 'plump ivory and rose-quartz elephants on parade, narrow rice-paper scrolls of black calligraphy in gilded wood frames, Buddha the Glutton immobilized under an ample lampshade of taut pink silk'.[8] This fragile and mysterious connection with China was soon severed abruptly. When Mildred finally came back to New York and her two children for good, it was as a widow, after Jack Rosenblatt died of pulmonary tuberculosis on 19 October 1938 in the German American Hospital in Tientsin, northern China. Susan was five years old.

How much could Susan have known or remembered about her father? In 'Notes of a Childhood' there are some scattered entries about 'Daddy', especially moving because of their scarcity. Susan remembered her father teaching her to whistle. She remembered him telling her to eat her parsley. 'Daddy showing me how he folded his handkerchief. (In their bedroom.)' 'Keeping Daddy's ring in a box'. 'Daddy's pigskin wallet'. 'Daddy singing'. 'Dreams of Daddy coming back, opening the ap't door'. 'Mom telling me Daddy is dead. In the living room.'[9]

On some level Susan blamed her mother for her father's death, and was unable to forgive her. Jack's death had an impossibly unfinished, abstract quality for Susan, at five or six, coming to full consciousness yet having so few memories of him. Her grief ripened slowly over years, tangled up with her thoughts about China, a half-imaginary place which both was and was not a legitimate part of her identity. In 'Notes of a Childhood' she recalls feeling jealousy towards someone else (Margie Rocklin) for having been born in China.[10] In the later, semi-fictional 'Project for a Trip to China', Susan relates that 'China inspired the first lie I remember telling. Entering the first grade, I told my classmates that I was born in China . . . I know that I wasn't born in China.'[11] 'Project for a Trip to China' was at one stage, in 1972, conceived as a whole book dedicated to Sontag's father, fusing meditations on China with fragments of narrative, stills from Lumière films, and photographs:

of Jack; of Karl Marx from a cover of *China News*; and a picture owned by Georges Bataille, taken in China in 1910, of a *lingchi* torture victim.[12] In the story Sontag reveals that her father was sixteen when he first visited China, and that Mildred was probably twenty-four. She describes a photograph of Jack, looking 'pleased, boyish, shy, absent', in a rickshaw in Tientsin in 1931, two years before she was born.[13] When she was ten years old, she writes, she dug a hole in the back yard of her house, 6 feet by 6 feet by 6 feet, as if she was trying to dig all the way to China. She covered it with 'eight-foot-long planks', and sat in it. By this time, 'the ivory and quartz elephants had been auctioned'; the hole was 'my refuge', 'my cell', 'my study', 'my grave'.[14]

The hole – also clearly a kind of grave for Susan's father, whose burial place she tells us she does not know and says, pointedly, even her mother has forgotten – seems potentially a fictional invention, but it is also mentioned in 'Notes of a Childhood', where she recalls 'digging it, filling it, digging it again' and where it is placed between two other memories loosely associated with China, and death: of a woman whose husband had tuberculosis, and a Chinese family with a grocery store in Tucson.[15] As 'Project for a Trip to China' suggests, the exotic, inconclusive quality of Jack's death in Susan's mind was also intertwined with fictionality, with telling stories, telling lies. Even the way Mildred broke the news to Susan, long after the event, had a certain staginess and concealment.

> After M. returned to the United States from China in early 1939, it took several months for her to tell me my father wasn't coming back. I was nearly through the first grade . . . I knew, when she asked me to come into the living room, that it was a solemn occasion . . . She was brief . . . I didn't cry long. I was already imagining how I would announce this new fact to my friends . . . I didn't really believe my father was dead.[16]

Mildred clearly found it hard to tell Susan about Jack's death; Susan never forgot this deception.[17]

Having a dead father, being a half-orphan, gave Susan a certain licence, not only to reimagine her father and idealize him but to reinvent herself and her past. This was good practice for a burgeoning writer; there was also an illicit freedom in this, as well as a confusing sadness. This was very early in life to be forging new beginnings out of endings. New beginnings would continue to be forged throughout her life, even as she herself faced death many decades later. And there was always a space left within her for hoping that endings were not endings or, more precisely, that her father's death was a fiction, not reality: 'I still weep in any movie with a scene in which a father returns home after a long desperate absence, at the moment when he hugs his child. Or children.'[18]

Mildred, meanwhile, only recently turned 30, found herself in radically changed, all-too-real circumstances after Jack's death, without a husband, with two young children. She was scarred; years later Susan wrote in her diaries that her mother came back from China 'a casualty of life'.[19] She was very likely depressed, as well as grieving, as she moved the family to several apartments and houses in New York and elsewhere. From Susan's accounts, the loss of a father and Mildred's return from China did not bring new closeness between mother and daughter, now sharing intimate domestic space. Mildred never listened to her, Susan came to feel, but at the same time craved her emotional support, making Susan into her friend and partner – even, Susan would write, her 'mother's *mother*', and Judith's mother too – more than her daughter.[20] But much of this came later. After hearing of her father's death, Susan's immediate reaction was to suffer from asthma attacks; following doctor's advice, Mildred moved to Miami, where the climate was to cure Susan. In 'Notes of a Childhood' Susan remembers asking her mother how to spell 'pneumonia' on the train to Florida, where they had coconut trees in their back yard.[21] Soon Mildred took the family, again for Susan's health, to Tucson, Arizona, which always remained, for Susan, '*imaginatively* my childhood'.[22]

Among the eight houses and apartments Susan remembers living in (in 'Pilgrimage') before the age of fourteen – she went to at least six schools before then, too – 'Notes of a Childhood' clusters several memories in an apartment in Forest Hills, Queens, New York. She recalled taking the bus to school from 68th Street, hearing Shostakovich's Fifth Symphony on the radio, and going to the theatre (she saw her second play, *Life with Father*, with her mother, at age eight). In 'Notes of a Childhood' she also remembered the 1939 New York World's Fair; listening to the Hit Parade with Rosie; buying a book on Chinese vases and crafts; reading *Les Misérables*; and writing an essay 'On Time' and a book on Russia – probably the 62-page manuscript 'Saga of the Soviets' by 'Sue Rosenblatt', one of several juvenile writings based on news reports of the Second World War.[23] Susan recalled 'hearing about "world war"' when she started school in September 1939 and feeling frightened when Uncle Aaron telephoned on 7 December 1941 about Pearl Harbour – Mildred was out at a ball game.[24] But for most of what Susan would call 'my desert childhood' in Arizona, the war was far away.[25]

In 1943, Mildred moved the family into a four-room bungalow, 2409 East Drachman, on a dirt road in Tucson on the edge of the University of Arizona. Susan shared a bedroom with Judith and remembered testing her little sister on American cities, at night from her upper bunk bed.[26] Although she later wrote of Tucson with a certain derision, especially in 'Pilgrimage', Susan thrived in the hot, dusty, arid, spiky tumbleweed streets around Drachman. Her lungs and health improved. At the local school, Mansfield Junior High, she was editor of *The Sparkler*, the school paper, and self-published *The Cactus Press*, a four-page newspaper filled

2409 East Drachman, the Bungalow in Tucson, Arizona, where Sontag grew up in the 1940s.

with stories, poems, plays and war reportage, using a hand mimeograph, her own primitive printing machine. She recalled riding around the neighbourhood on her bicycle selling the newspaper for 5 cents. In Tucson she also started writing her journals, beginning a lifelong, essential habit. The diaries did not have an auspicious opening: the first entry, Susan later noted, was on seeing the rotting corpse of a dog by the road. Although they didn't really get going for several years, the diaries saw the young Susan beginning to sense and test her potential as a writer. In their pages of lists and aphorisms, notes and sketches, reflections and aspirations, assessments and exhortations – and, soon, of love affairs – she would build herself up as if from scratch, and claw her way out of the desert.

She was also by this time, as she would be for the rest of her life, a voracious reader. From her earliest days, books were her escape, her identity, her 'household deities', her 'spaceships'.[27] Yet she was never a passive reader; she read her way into the life that she would lead. She later claimed to have begun reading at age three and to have read, at six, a biography of Marie Curie written by her daughter, which gave Susan a fierce desire to be a chemist (she improvised a chemistry lab in the bungalow). She progressed from this early enthusiasm to wanting to be a doctor. What else was she reading? 'Pilgrimage' gives an idea of her range:

> Fairy tales and comics (my comics collection was vast), Compton's Encyclopaedia, the Bobbsey Twins and other Stratemeyer series, books about astronomy, chemistry, China, biographies of scientists, all of Richard Halliburton's travel books, and a fair number of mostly Victorian-era classics. Then, drifting to the rear of a stationery and greeting-card store in the village that was downtown Tucson in the mid-nineteen-forties, I toppled into the deep well of the Modern Library. Here were standards, and here, at the back of each book, was my first list. I had only to acquire and read (ninety-five cents for the small ones, a dollar twenty-five for the Giants) – my sense of possibility unfolding, with each book, like a carpenter's rule.[28]

This was only a sample. Around this time Susan also devoured the work of Edgar Allan Poe and two formative novels about the writing life: Louisa May Alcott's *Little Women* and Jack London's *Martin Eden*. In early adolescence she would read two other books which exerted an enormous influence on her, André Gide's *Journals* and Thomas Mann's *The Magic Mountain* – and was reading or planning to read Apollinaire, Dante, Dostoevsky, Faulkner, Hawthorne, Huysmans, Kafka, Melville, Rilke, Rimbaud, Verlaine; and plays by Hellman, O'Neill, Shaw and Synge. The gates were slowly opening; Susan would read her way through a good deal of the American and European canon during the next few years, albeit with many gaps, favouring the European writers, as she would for the rest of her life, while also savouring nineteenth-century American fiction.

The realities she craved from books were intrinsically unlike the world in which she grew up. She read to travel, to be elsewhere – in the bungalow, Susan formed the 'Drachman Travel Bureau' by collecting information from Chambers of Commerce across America – and travel, or the idea of travel, would remain an obsession throughout her life. In the childhood milieu of Tucson in the 1940s, 'reading produced its blissful, confirming alienations',[29] and in all of Susan's accounts of Arizona, loneliness seeps through, alongside a sense that she was killing time while she waited to grow up and live the life she wanted. Apart from her visits to the stationery store, with its few but welcome books, the best amusement Susan found in Tucson, as she wrote in 'Pilgrimage' – whose earlier title was 'Doing Time' – was to walk out on the Old Spanish Trail towards the foothills, 'examine close up the fiercest saguaros and prickly pears, scrutinize the ground for arrowheads and snakes, pocket pretty rocks, imagine being lost or a sole survivor, wish I were an Indian'.[30]

While Susan wanted to be elsewhere, one senses that Mildred did too, and often was. She was seeing another man, Nathan Sontag, or 'Nat', whom she married in 1945. Handsome, upbeat and enthusiastic, Nathan was a pilot with the U.S. Army Air Forces who had been shot down five days after D-Day and sent to the desert to recuperate after a year in hospital. Having lost her father in a never-visited China, Susan gained a surrogate who seemed to have fallen out of the sky. Now out of uniform, he was a fond stepfather, and Susan, who found herself sometimes bragging about his military prowess, was glad for his stabilizing influence on her mother, which gave Susan even more freedom to roam. She wrote under Nat's surname for the rest of her life. But, reading 'Pilgrimage', it is not hard to see Susan's scorn and pain deriving from her inability to find any credible role for herself in life at home once Nat moved in, punctuated by barbecues and driving lessons. Judith, on the contrary, relished her suburban American girlhood. For the older Susan the most appealing prospect, indeed the only future, was in orchestrating her escape from this newly formed – 'too late!' – 'family' nest.[31]

In 1946, Nathan, Mildred, Judith and Susan moved to 'a cozy shuttered cottage with rosebush hedges and three birch trees at the entrance of the San Fernando Valley' in California (Susan invests the word 'cozy' with special malice).[32] If Tucson was always, for Susan, her childhood, then with this final family move to California, when she was thirteen, it was already ending. On the West Coast, Susan's horizons broadened in the shelter of Los Angeles, a haven in the 1940s not only for Hollywood directors and stars but European émigrés devoted to high Modernist culture who had fled wartime Europe for the incongruities of LA's neo-Bauhaus architecture, movie palaces, beaches and lemon trees: exiled composers Susan idolized (Stravinsky, Schoenberg) and writers (Mann, Brecht, Isherwood, Huxley). That these great luminaries were inaccessible scarcely mattered; she was aware of their presence, grew up in their glow and identified, to whatever slight degree, with their distance from – in spite of proximity to – the mainstream American culture of the period.

More practically, Susan now had her own room. After being sent to bed she could shut the door and read for hours by flashlight without having to hide under the covers. And she lived near a good bookstore: the Pickwick, on Hollywood Boulevard, where she browsed, bought and sometimes stole books. She entered North Hollywood High School, but her real education was taking place in downtown Los Angeles, among the one- and two-storey buildings within a few blocks of the crossroads of Hollywood Boulevard and Highland Avenue. Most afternoons, once school was over, she took the Red Car, not home to the San Fernando Valley, but downtown. As well as the Pickwick, here was a record store where she spent hours each week in the listening booths, and an international news-stand with literary magazines, including

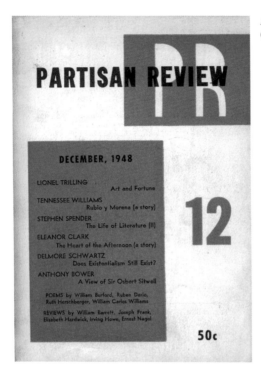

Partisan Review
(December 1948).

Partisan Review, Kenyon Review, Politics and *Horizon*. 'Soon I was sipping at a hundred straws', Sontag wrote, looking back on these discoveries made while out hunting 'treasure'.[33] At the same news-stand she first read 'Art and Fortune' by Lionel Trilling, and glimpsed her future. 'I just began to tremble with excitement . . . from then on, my dream was to grow up, move to New York and write for *Partisan Review*.'[34] She now had an unusually well-developed sense of vocation. She knew who she wanted to be, where she wanted to be. In her diaries Susan set herself, with tremendous will and desire, towards her goal, writing schedules, reading lists and self-prescriptions; scolding herself, training herself, consoling herself.

At North Hollywood High she edited the school newspaper *The Arcade*, writing editorials and reviews of the films from the nearby 'dream factory', now signing her name 'Sue Sontag'. On the outside, the thirteen-to-fifteen-year-old 'Sue' was an assiduous, stern student, militantly self-improving. In her high school yearbook photograph she looks every part the 'Goody Two-Shoes' her mother said she was – an 'appalling accusation', the later Sontag wrote.[35] But she was also learning not only how to improve herself, but how to let go. In 'Pilgrimage' Sontag writes of her new companions, Elaine (Levi) and Mel (Roseman), both older than her, mentors who shared her passion for classical composers and the Monday chamber-music series 'Evenings on the Roof' at the Wilshire Ebell Theatre. This was also a place for romantic liaisons. Sontag recalled having her first kiss at a Roof concert; she also went to summer concerts at the Hollywood Bowl, getting in free by working as an usher.

Sontag's high school yearbook photograph at North Hollywood High, 1949.

Her first boyfriend was Peter Haidu. They bonded initially over their lost fathers and shared love of European culture, after meeting in the school cafeteria. Peter's father had been arrested by the Gestapo in the early years of the Second World War. With his mother, he escaped from wartime Paris to Lisbon, then to New York in 1941. Susan and Peter held hands and wept through foreign movies at a theatre they discovered called the Laurel; they went bicycling in the canyons and 'rolled about, embracing, in the weeds'. He was 'dark-haired, skinny, nervous' and, crucially, taller than her. She wrote: 'A boyfriend had to be not just a best friend but taller, and only Peter qualified.' But there was strain in Sontag's affections. For by this time she was also acutely, painfully aware of her physical attraction to women.

In the very public pages of 'Pilgrimage', the liaison with Peter segues into a crush on another boy, Merrill: a '"dreamboat"', although shorter than her. In her mother's Pontiac or Merrill's parents' Chevy they parked at night on the rim of Mulholland Drive, 'the great plain of twinkling lights below like an endless airport', talking about music.[36] Like the relationship with Peter, Sontag portrays her trysts with Merrill as a shared set of enthusiasms.

'Pilgrimage' ends in 1949 without a word about Sontag's love for women. But in her diaries, Sontag's early struggles with her sexuality reached a great crisis and liberation as a teenager, especially once she left home. After graduation from North Hollywood High, Sontag went to the University of California, Berkeley, in early 1949. Berkeley was a compromise to appease Mildred, who did not want her daughter to go too far away. Now sixteen, Sontag read gratefully, greedily there: Huxley's *Point Counter Point*, Dostoevsky's *The Brothers Karamazov*, Hesse, Steiner, Hopkins, Eliot. Unnerved by her 'lesbian tendencies' she tried to persuade herself to be attracted to men rather than – or as well as – women. By April that year, Sontag was in love (one-sidedly, it seems) with Irene Lyons, and yet wanted to prove to herself 'at least, that I am bisexual', by also experimenting with men. On the cover of her journal for May 1949, Sontag wrote in capitals that she had been 'REBORN' in the period recounted in that diary.[37]

The journal recounts two relationships at Berkeley. The first is with a man, Al, or Allan Cox. Al was handsome, intelligent and talkative, yet for all their intimacy Sontag felt little physical attraction to him. In March, however, she met Harriet Sohmers, who worked at the Campus Textbook Exchange. Harriet was tall, Susan wrote, attractive, with a lovely smile, wonderfully alive.[38] Susan was sharp, stylish, sure of herself, but more sexually naive than Harriet. After their first meeting at the campus bookstore where, Harriet recalled, she flirtatiously recommended Susan read Djuna Barnes's *Nightwood*,[39] they often talked on Saturday mornings after a class on the 'Age of Samuel Johnson'. When Harriet invited Susan to come with her to some bars in San Francisco, Susan accepted. They took the F train one Saturday evening. Thus began a long – and, for Susan, eye-opening – night, which started with a Chinese meal before Harriet took Susan to several gay bars: Mona's, where she was introduced to a group of Harriet's friends; the Paper Doll; and 12 Adler. In the early hours of the morning they crossed over the Golden Gate Bridge to Sausalito, where Susan and Harriet ended up sharing a bed and making love, to Susan's great delight.

Sontag's early relationships with men had been cerebral affairs, reinforcing the side of her that wanted an academic career. An oppressive sense of doing the right thing, even a mild revulsion, accompanied many of them. The relationship with Harriet was nothing less than a revelation. It awakened Sontag emotionally, sexually, intellectually. Her interest was rekindled in everything at once, as she vowed ecstatically in her diaries: '*everything matters!*'[40] Simultaneously, she decided against taking up the academic life, as if heterosexuality and her life with men was associated with academia and good behaviour, and her life with women linked with a more freely roaming intellectuality and sensuality. She still had many decisions to make on all these scores; after all, she was only sixteen.

At the end of May 1949, Sontag won a scholarship for a BA at the University of Chicago, where she had always really wanted to go. Harriet left for New York in mid-June. Susan went home to the San Fernando Valley, taking a holiday job as a filing clerk in an insurance office. There was a summer affair with another woman, 'L'. In September, she headed east by train for Chicago, a two-day trip, making impressionistic travel notes in her diary.

Trying to express the intellectual intensity of the environment at Chicago, Sontag later described the university as 'a total situation, a benevolent dictatorship'.[41] Though she had been reading gluttonously for years, at Chicago she discovered more structured ways of reading and thinking. Joseph Schwab, whose philosophy course 'Observation, Interpretation, Integration' Sontag took twice, was one inspirational mentor. Kenneth Burke was another. Sontag had been reading Burke's criticism for years and knew his novel, *Towards a Better Life*. She remembered Burke spending three months going through Joseph Conrad's *Victory* line by line; he was also thrillingly full of anecdotes about the writing life in Greenwich Village in the 1920s, with stories about Djuna Barnes and Hart Crane. Also important to Sontag were philosophy seminars by Richard McKeon and Leo Strauss, on Aristotle, Machiavelli, Nietzsche and others. She wrote a dissertation on *Nightwood*. She went to concerts, films, the Art Institute, the opera. Swamped as she was in new intellectual stimuli, the nascent creative writer in her lay dormant; Chicago turned her more into a critic.

The pivotally disillusioning meeting with Thomas Mann, recounted in 'Pilgrimage' as having taken place in 1947, when Sontag was fourteen, also appears in fragmentary form in her diaries of December 1949, during her time at Chicago. Where in the memoir the trip to visit Mann is with Merrill only, in the diaries 'E, F, and I' visit Mann – or 'God' – at his home in LA on 1550 San Remo Drive.[42] While in 'Pilgrimage' Sontag emphasizes her unwillingness to pay her idol a fan visit, stressing that it was Merrill's idea, the diary notes show that she knew it was important enough to write about. In 'Pilgrimage' the event occurs deep in her youth and is presented as embarrassing in its naivety. Turning the memory into a memoir, the smoothness of several details – such as the conflation of 'E' and 'F' into 'Merrill' – suggests either a heavily reworked scene, or that much was blurred and half-forgotten by the time Sontag came to write about it again in the 1980s.

In the memoir, Susan and Merrill arrive at four o'clock, and first see Mann in his study, impressively set behind a 'massive, ornate dark table';[43] in the diary notes, 'E, F, and I' arrive at six and find Mann on the couch in the living room holding his dog, before going into his study. In both versions he wears a beige suit and looks uncannily the same as his author photographs. In both versions, they talk about similar things. In 'Pilgrimage', however, Mann also asks Susan and Merrill about their own reading, to Susan's dismay, and is surprised at their European tastes (Romain Rolland, Joyce's *Portrait*, Kafka's 'Metamorphosis') and lack of interest in American writers. What persists in both versions is the disappointment of meeting a great writer. Sontag does not spare herself, stressing her impertinence, her gaucheness, her garishly American, uncouth nature. But this brief encounter with 'God' brings on a momentary loss of faith. The interview with Mann inverts, in a way, the great moment of religious epiphany of so many nineteenth-century autobiographies; the greatest moment of vision in Sontag's early diaries, meanwhile, is her night out in San Francisco with Harriet.

Early in her second and last year at Chicago, on the advice of a friend, Sontag attended a section of the 'Social Science II' course,

Thomas Mann
in 1949.

on Freud's *Civilization and Its Discontents* and *Moses and Monotheism*,
being given by a young instructor, Philip Rieff. As the story has
been told, she arrived late for Rieff's seminar one winter morning
in 1950, and strode to the back of the class. She was the last to leave.
Rieff asked her name, and if she would have lunch with him. In her
diary for 21 November 1950, Sontag noted that she had been offered
an exciting opportunity – 'to *do* some research work' for Philip
Rieff. By 2 December, they were married. She was seventeen; he
was twenty-eight. The only surviving notebook entry for 1951,
from 3 January, is succinct: 'I marry Philip with full consciousness
+ fear of my will toward self-destructiveness.'[44] The notebooks
which had chronicled Susan's relations with Harriet and others
so enthusiastically would now fall almost silent for several years
– unless many pages have been destroyed or lost. A new phase

was now beginning, and there might not have been the time, the privacy or the desire, for the moment, to write it all down. Having left her mother, sister, and stepfather far behind her in Los Angeles, Susan was now about to start a family of her own.

2

Notes on Marriage, 1951–1958

Sontag's sudden marriage was an enigma even to her, only half explained away by the swiftness with which it was begun. In the diaries, after the agonies over sexuality and the exultant sense of rebirth and revelation Sontag felt after her early lesbian experiences, the engagement to Philip Rieff reads as a tremendous, gloriously foolish, rash act of self-persuasion and hopeful drama. Marrying after only a few days of acquaintance, Sontag, always romantically earnest, never cynical in affairs of the heart, must not have doubted her passion, must have desired to be completely swept away. And there was a logic, for her, to impulsiveness: she felt that love struck instantly – 'seizes one' – so why wait?[1]

Yet the cryptic diary reference to her 'self-destructiveness' vis-à-vis the marriage also hints that part of the decision to actually marry came out of panicked self-awareness, self-delusion, anxiety, fear that if she didn't stop her female relationships now – 'no more women, no more bars', as 'F' had told her in 1949 – she would never manage it.[2] She might have felt she was young enough at seventeen to change completely. She had a very strong desire to be 'normal', which was almost but not quite as fierce as her desire for self-realization. Also behind the decision to marry Philip Rieff was Sontag's wish to flee from her background and family into a new life. Having waited so long to escape her childhood, in Chicago Sontag rushed headlong into adulthood, partly to ensure she would never have to go back to Los Angeles. She never did return to live on the West Coast.

Philip Rieff at
the University of
Pennsylvania, 1968.

Philip Rieff was born in Chicago in 1922 and had grown up in
the city, graduating from the university in 1946 before becoming an
instructor. He had a formidable reputation and was rather austere
and formal; Sontag felt, at first, slightly in awe of this man who
had such a commanding presence in the seminar room and shared
many of her own intellectual obsessions, including Kafka and
Freud. For so many years of her childhood she had been desperate
for intelligent company, and had found companionship with Peter,
Merrill, Elaine, Mel, Harriet. Now she had met Philip, who 'talked
and talked'.[3] 'We had great talks, Philip and I', Sontag told another
'Philip', Phillip Lopate, much later: 'We would talk together for
hours. I remember we went to a party, and afterwards we drove

home and sat in the car discussing everyone. Then the sun came up and it was morning and we realized we had been sitting there all night!'[4] A variation on the same anecdote also appears in a short story, 'The Letter Scene', from 1986, alongside other memories of 'the delirious amity of non-stop talking' of Sontag's marriage. 'I was, you see, so *used* to him', she wrote:

> I felt safe. I didn't feel like a separate person . . . we never separated for more than a few hours, just the time he taught his classes and I took mine – we were insatiable.[5]

Shortly after they were married, Susan and Philip shared an apartment together at 6227 Ingleside Avenue in Chicago. Susan finished her BA in 1951, and that summer the couple went to Europe together, sailing on the *Newfoundland* from Boston, where they moved to when Rieff took up an assistant professorship at Brandeis University the following year. By the beginning of 1952, Susan was pregnant; they were living in Cambridge, in a house in Harvard Yard, when their son David was born that September. It was a difficult birth, and Sontag stayed in bed for a month afterwards, just as Mildred had also stayed in bed for a month after Susan's birth.[6] Susan's Irish nanny Rosie was enlisted to help nurse David, in another mirroring of Susan's own childhood. Yet the world into which David was born – intellectually driven, surrounded by discussions on literature, philosophy, mythology and religion – could not have been further from Sontag's youth in New York and Arizona. Susan was, inevitably, very busy mothering David for the next few years. But, in the cocoon of her academic marriage, in her early twenties, she also learned how to write, how to argue, how to hold her own; at Harvard during this period the couple frequently entertained or were entertained by other intellectuals, including the philosophers Aron Gurwitsch and Herbert Marcuse and the historian E. H. Carr.

Sontag enrolled in a master's programme in English at the University of Connecticut in 1953, although she left after a year, switching to read English at Harvard before enrolling in the philosophy department there as a graduate student in 1955, soon beginning a doctorate on comparative religion, modern philosophy and literature. At Harvard, Sontag was particularly influenced by the theologian Paul Tillich and the charismatic, intense émigré professor of religion Jacob Taubes, an expert on Gnosticism, whose wife, also called Susan, became a close friend. Beautiful, exotic-looking, with dark hair and a long, narrow face, Susan Taubes was in Sontag's mind her doppelgänger, sharing her first name: 'ma sosie (*'my double'*)'.[7] Tillich and Jacob Taubes were also part of the wave of Jewish refugee intellectuals whose teachings Sontag later remembered as a central tier of her education: she

Jacob and Susan
Taubes, *c.* 1949.

also included Hannah Arendt, Gershom Scholem, Marcuse and Gurwitsch among these figures.

After the single, ominous diary entry for 1951 about her marriage, there was nothing at all the year of David's birth; but in 1953 Sontag's surviving diaries show small signs of life, with entries about being in the bookshop at Cambridge and browsing through Kafka; accounts of excruciatingly pleasurable dreams; notes on style – and on avoiding dialogue in the stories she was writing at the time, which indicates that as well as criticism, Sontag was also writing fiction. The following two years likewise have only a few diary pages; but in 1956 Sontag begins a series of fragmentary diary notes on marriage, which strike a deeply personal chord among the other entries on Gnosticism, Tolstoy, philosophy, religion, Henry James, Kant, Lucretius, Kierkegaard. The closed, cloistered academic life Susan was leading in the 1950s was far from satisfying all her needs. In supplanting one family with another, she had locked herself in to another repressive space, another family she needed to escape from. 'In marriage, every desire becomes a decision', Sontag wrote in September 1956. Then, in November:

> A Project – Notes on Marriage
> Marriage is based on the principle of *inertia*.
> Unloving proximity.
> Marriage is all private – no public – behavior . . .
> The leakage of talk in marriage.
> (My marriage, anyway.)[8]

Six years in to her marriage to Philip Rieff, with David now four, Sontag was dissatisfied. Even the talk she had sought and loved so keenly was now seen as merely 'leakage'. Interspersed with the 'Notes on Marriage', Sontag also began another theme, 'Notes on Interpretation', as if the two subjects – and her growing rejection of them – were conjoined, linked by an excess of talk, speculation, deliberation, and an insufficiency of spontaneity, passion, life. Sontag wrote early in 1957 that she had not felt free during the last six years.[9] This sense of her lack of freedom was exacerbated by a trip to New York, taken after Christmas in 1956 with David (handed over to Rosie on arrival), where she stayed up all night at a party given by the poet Richard Eberhart, meeting Gregory Corso and Allen Ginsberg. On her return to the staid precincts of Harvard, she recorded a terrifying dream around the turn of 1957, in which a horse moved up behind her as she went down a flight of stairs into a swimming pool, putting its front legs over her shoulders. She screamed, unable to remove the weight, and sank down. That she had a slight phobia of water, attributed to an early incident when her Uncle Sonny took her swimming too far out, only adds resonance to the nightmare.[10]

Throughout the mid- to late 1950s, husband and wife worked together on a study of Sigmund Freud, which became Philip Rieff's first book, *Freud: The Mind of the Moralist* (1959). Rieff had submitted his doctoral thesis, on Freud's contribution to political philosophy, at the University of Chicago in 1954, but writing his first book he was frequently blocked, needing his young wife's help. Although Susan never took Philip's surname when they married, remaining 'Susan Sontag', the first edition of his book ends its acknowledgements with a dedication to 'my wife, Susan Rieff', who 'devoted herself unstintingly to this book'.[11] In later years, however, Susan said she had written the whole thing. 'Although her name did not appear on the cover, she was a full co-author, she always said', Sigrid Nunez writes in her memoir, *Sempre Susan* (2011). 'In fact, she sometimes went further, claiming to have written the entire book herself, "every single word of it".'[12] It is impossible for any reader of Sontag's later work to read *Freud: The Mind of the Moralist* without seeing her style in it, and many of her themes. Rieff, an expert on Freud, was responsible for much of the book, despite what Sontag says, but the voice and concerns of her later work come through unmistakably. Either Rieff had such an influence on Sontag that all her subsequent writing reads like the Freud book, or her own contribution to the Freud book was so substantial that it can be fairly regarded as her own, at least, as much as Rieff's.

In his review in *Encounter*, the critic Philip Toynbee found the writing in *Freud* so high in quality that he reproduced a 'long necklace' of quotations. These were charged with the aphoristic, epigrammatic bite so typical of Sontag's later critical writing. 'Mr Rieff writes quite exceptionally well', Toynbee commented, furnishing his list of disconnected, floating quotes:

> Conscience, not passion, emerges as the last enemy of reason. . . . the alternative explanation always lurking at the edge of every psychoanalytic interpretation . . .

> Indeed, because in his case-histories Freud never *reported* but *interpreted* them, what passes for description in Freud is already judgement.

> All experience is symptomatic now . . .

> Such careful and detailed concentration on the self as Freud encourages may more often produce pedants of the inner life than virtuosi of the outer one.

> In the emergent democracy of the sick, everyone can to some extent play doctor to others, and none is allowed the temerity to claim that he can definitely cure or be cured. The hospital is succeeding the church and the parliament as the archetypal institution of Western culture.[13]

The theme of Sontag's first book of essays, *Against Interpretation* (1966), is here in the scepticism about the endless alternative explanations in Freudian analysis; the moral of Sontag's first novel, *The Benefactor* (1963), in the dangers of 'such careful and detailed concentration on the self' producing 'pedants of the inner life'; and analogies explored in *Illness as Metaphor* (1978) – which opens with the statement 'illness is the night-side of life, a more onerous citizenship'[14] – are here in 'the emergent democracy of the sick'.

Freud has similar echoes and affinities on nearly every page. Its focus, dealing with the ethical implications of Freud's thought, aligns with a lifelong theme of Sontag's oeuvre: the tussle between ethics and aesthetics. More broadly, the terrain of Freud's writings, encompassing all of Emerson's list of subjects thought inexplicable in his day, as Rieff (and Sontag) wrote in the preface to *Freud* – 'language, sleep, madness, dreams, beasts, sex' – was arguably more influential for Sontag in her early formation as a fiction writer than the work of any novelist, except Kafka.[15] Freud's revelation of the unconscious, the instincts and the irrational opened up a rich space for fictional invention which Sontag would explore at length, above all in her first two novels.

Yet *Freud* was also quietly subversive. It conveyed deep knowledge and respect for Freud's achievement, while dismantling his ideas and techniques. It is tempting to hear Sontag's voice in its criticisms of Freud, rather than its praise. Sontag's later tone and arguments flicker especially strongly across the pages of an early chapter on 'The Tactics of Interpretation', tackling the way in which, for Freud, nothing is ever allowed to be just what it is. 'Slips of the tongue, pen, memory; mislaying of objects; fiddling or doodling; random naming and numbering – the most ordinary trivialities may become symptomatic, meaningful.' One thing is always substituted for another by Freud, Rieff (and Sontag) suggest – yet with how much accuracy? Did Freudian analysis not encourage merely 'an excess of digging, in which what is significant becomes simply what is underneath'?[16]

Freud is likewise gently ironic about how the master psychoanalyst so often exempted himself from his own theories and techniques – he alone, Rieff (and Sontag) dryly observe, reserved the right to interpret his own dreams. More generally, the analytic session is intrinsically random, Sontag (surely just her, here) writes, comparing it to the Dadaist Kurt Schwitters and his *Merz* works of the 1920s, made from 'gutter-pickings in a single city block': 'as a time limit the analyst's daily hour is no less arbitrary.'[17] The critique gathers pace as *Freud* continues. Freud never attended sufficiently to the problems of analysis being a purely verbal medium; his welcome openness towards sexuality is marred by his misogyny and patronizing attitude towards women; his psychology never becomes fully social, indeed is intrinsically self-obsessed.

Freud's views on marriage likewise offer little compensation for Rieff (and Sontag), since in Freud's view physical tenderness and mental affection turn into hostilities. 'Freud judged married love among the middle classes impossible', write the young, middle-class married couple. Quoting Freud, Sontag (again surely just her) interrupts with just one word in precis, as if alluding to her own marriage:

'Under the spiritual disappointment and physical deprivation which thus becomes the fate of most marriages, both partners find themselves reduced again to their pre-conjugal condition' – abstinence – 'but poorer by the loss of an illusion.'[18]

Throughout the writing of *Freud*, Sontag and Rieff's own marriage came under strain, and moved towards breaking point. Sontag felt great passion for Rieff in the first year of their union, despite the pattern of her previous relations with other men.[19] But in her reckonings of the marriage, the decline had already begun after this first year. She did not act on her growing dissatisfactions for some time, no doubt because of David. Oddly, the decision to do so came around the same time that work on *Freud* was drawing to a close. Even when the decision to make the split was made, its enactment felt to Sontag like a slow-motion dream. She turned to her diaries to chronicle it, perhaps to mentally pinch herself, to show herself that this was really happening. And in some ways for some time it was a dream, in that only she was aware of it – Sontag eased herself over the precipice slowly, then lowered herself down alone, rope still in hand, long before telling Rieff and severing the bond. In early 1957 the fragmented notes on marriage in the diaries became more final. 'On marriage. That's all there is.'[20] She booked her escape: a ticket on the Holland America Line leaving from Hoboken, an eight-day voyage across the Atlantic. The ticket was $260.[21]

Sontag had applied to Oxford for a fellowship to continue her studies in philosophy for the academic year of 1957–8, and it had been awarded to her. When Philip was offered a fellowship at Stanford during the same period, the prospect of a temporary split became more clear-cut. David, about to turn five, would be looked after by Philip's family in Chicago. Leaving David was perhaps the hardest part of the decision. Sontag had lost her own father at five; now David would be losing his mother at around the same age, if only for a year (and subsequently, to some degree, his father too).

The parting of ways between Sontag and Rieff in the summer of 1957 was fraught. This, as David himself notes, was effectively the end of the marriage, but it was not acknowledged as such at the time.[22] Both partners seemed to know what was happening, yet it was shrouded in a haze of unreality: this was a brief separation, not an end. 'Since we were going to be married forever we had granted me a sabbatical', Sontag wrote in 'The Letter Scene'.[23]

But there were arguments and embraces and, on the final night, Sontag went to sleep in David's bed when he awoke at dawn and cried out. Philip finished packing the car later in the morning and drove himself and his son to the grandparents' house. In a lightly fictionalized narrative in her diaries, with Sontag as 'Lee' (Susan's middle name) and Philip as 'Martin' (Philip's younger brother's name), Susan rewrote the last days in Cambridge, and the decisions leading up to it: Lee's desire to go away to travel in Europe for a year; Martin's wanting to finish 'the book' that year before they both applied for positions abroad; Lee's reluctance, inability, to wait. Possibly, Sontag was contemplating writing this all up at some stage as an autobiographical novel.

In the normal day-by-day log of the diaries, meanwhile, the last days in Cambridge are described in a feverishly over-excited way, stretching to several pages per day, suggesting that if Philip was not aware of the momentousness of events, then Susan was. Uncharacteristically, she listed things almost by the hour, noting how she and Philip never said goodbye properly amid the preparations and how, in fact, they stopped quarrelling only by stopping talking. Left alone after Philip and David had gone, Susan didn't know what to do with her freedom at first, in the silence of the exit of her family. The entries over the next few days are excited, fearful, frenzied, as she moved between packing, writing and correcting parts of *Freud*, eating snacks, seeing her philosophy professor, watching films and reading, in preparation for her European sojourn, Hemingway's *The Sun Also Rises* ('dull'). She was trying to write a philosophy paper, but couldn't maintain interest. She was so consumed by restlessness, pacing around the house, that she walked miles indoors in these few days, she thought.[24] Yet when she finally left for New York on 3 September, she was nearly late arriving at the station that afternoon, only just catching the train in time. She was to depart by ship for England two days later.

On her last morning in New York she had breakfast with Peter Haidu, then studying for an MA at Columbia, and there was a last-minute rush to reach the docks for the 11:30 sailing time. She found Jacob Taubes at the gangplank of the ship to see her off – he had been waiting for an hour and waved after the boat until it was out of sight. Sontag found she was too jittery to stand on deck and watch the New York skyline. The crossing would take more than a week: enough time to reflect on what she had done. On arrival in England, Susan saw some sights in London with a friend, Jane Degras, with whom she also went on a brief trip to Florence in the last week of September.

There are glimpses of Sontag during her brief time at St Anne's College, Oxford, in an autobiographical novel, *Her Own Terms* (1988), by one of her fellow students, Judith Grossman, in which she appears as an exotic, displaced specimen, desirable, self-assured, dressed all in black, obscure and mysterious – especially concerning her past, and the husband and son she had left behind in America, the fact of which surprised and shocked her contemporaries when they heard of it. At 24, on her own, studying philosophy, Sontag did not seem obviously like a mother; her time at Oxford was a kind of play-acting in which she was a 'real', carefree, unattached student. She did not take Oxford that seriously; her relative maturity and experience, despite her age, made her feel apart from the other students. She attended philosophy classes taught by J. L. Austin; A. J. Ayer and Iris Murdoch were also teaching at Oxford at this time. But the atmosphere was too similar to what she had left behind.

At the end of 1957 she made another startling break, moving to Paris, continuing her philosophy studies at the Sorbonne. 'I was drifting away, discovering life was actually possible without him', Sontag wrote of her husband and this period in 'The Letter Scene'. 'But I did write, each evening.'[25] Philip, in America, encouraged her, saying Paris would be fun. As Susan's friend Annette Michelson realized, when Susan told her of Philip's acquiescence, Philip was inadvertently "'cutting his own throat'".[26]

Paris in 1957 and '58 was full of interesting figures. At the Sorbonne, Sontag went to hear Simone de Beauvoir – whose *The Second Sex* she had read in 1952 while pregnant with David – talking on the novel and its possibilities. She went to her first properly Parisian (rather than expatriate) intellectual cocktail party in February, at the philosopher Jean Wahl's beautiful apartment in the rue Le Peletier, where, she noted, there was a man who resembled Jean-Paul Sartre.[27] No doubt Sontag absorbed the ideological battles being fought by Maurice Merleau-Ponty, Louis Althusser, Claude Lévi-Strauss and Roland Barthes. But given the glacial progress of her thesis, now on 'the metaphysical suppositions of ethics', she was losing interest in philosophy, finding more inspiration in other arts.[28]

In Paris, she was extremely interested in the theatre, and she saw and wrote diary notes on plays by Luigi Pirandello (*Enrico IV*, *Ce soir on improvise*), Jean Racine (*Britannicus*), Bertolt Brecht (*The Caucasian Chalk Circle*) and Jean Genet (*Les Bonnes*).[29] She also began her habit of avid cinema-going, taking in films of all kinds, high- and low-brow, sometimes several in a day, absorbing the new work being done by François Truffaut, Jean-Luc Godard and Robert Bresson. She was blown away by Jean Rouch's film *Les Maîtres fous*, about the Hauka cult in Accra, Stroheim's *Foolish Wives* and Marcel Carné's *Les Enfants du Paradis*, which almost made her burst into tears.[30] She read novels by Nathanael West (*The Dream Life of Balso Snell*) and Italo Svevo (*The Confessions of Zeno*), and became aware of the *nouveau roman* then being expounded and practised by Alain Robbe-Grillet, Michel Butor and Nathalie Sarraute, as well as work by Emil Cioran, Michel Leiris and Georges Bataille.

Sontag was still living and absorbing experiences more than she was writing. But in her diaries soon after arrival on the Left

Bank, where she found a room on the rue Jacob, she started writing pen sketches of the mostly expatriate people she was meeting in Paris, who were all following the 'café routine' of Saint-Germain-des-Prés: cruising several cafés each evening after spending the day writing or painting. As Sontag portrays them, this was a weirdly glamorous, slightly damaged crowd; her mini-biographies, of a few lines each, often see through her subjects in a glance. She would always be able to size people up rapidly. Her reactions were often polarized. If she liked someone, she could be voluble, confessional, an instant friend and admirer; if not, she trained herself to be harder. In Paris, due to the double life she was leading – as the increasingly plaintive and demanding letters arriving from Philip in America reminded her – she also became aware of the mask of social relations. More than in Oxford, and differently, she was living her life as on a stage. Her past and present were disjointed; in the crack between them was space for self-invention. Irv Jaffe remembers Sontag picking up the proofs of *Freud* at the American Express office: another chapter nearly closed.[31]

Sontag's verbal gallery of her café life in Saint-Germain homes in especially on characters with complicated pasts and reinvented identities. There was 'J', a French Jew in his late twenties, always drunk or high, who kept his white powder in a bottle, had an illegitimate child and had lost both parents in concentration camps; Herta Haussmann, a German painter with a Hungarian boyfriend and an atelier in Montparnasse; Elliott Stein, Paris correspondent for the London-based *Opera*, a cinephile and connoisseur of kitsch whose tastes would influence Sontag's essay 'Notes on "Camp"'; Iris Owens, a 28-year-old New Yorker who had written five pornographic novels under the pseudonym 'Harriet Daimler', formerly married, now with a Greek sculptor; Ricardo Vigón, a young Cuban who wrote poetry and translated into Spanish at UNESCO; Sam Wolfenstein, a mathematician with a large collection

Harriet and Susan in Paris, 1958. Susan is in the middle, Harriet on the far right.

of books; Allen Ginsberg and his boyfriend Peter Orlovsky, staying at what became the 'Beat Hotel' at 9 rue Gît-le-Coeur.

And then there was Harriet Sohmers. Susan had contacted her before she came to Paris. Harriet had recently been involved in a relationship with the Cuban painter and soon-to-be-playwright María Irene Fornés, living with her at the Hôtel de Poitou on the rue de Seine before Fornés had returned to New York. In Paris, rather like Jean Seberg in Godard's *A bout de souffle* – perhaps Godard had seen the young, tall, dynamic, American girl about town – Harriet was working for the *New York Herald Tribune*; she had also done translations, including Sade's *Justine*, for the publisher Maurice Girodias, of Obelisk and later Olympia Press, which famously produced pornographic works as well as avant-garde texts such as Beckett's *Watt* and Nabokov's *Lolita*.[32]

Harriet's own memories of her time in Paris are nostalgic:

In Paris in the fifties, for a few years, we led a lovely life . . .
I worked at the *Tribune* in Paris, hours six to midnight, six nights
a week. Perfect schedule for the night person I was then. After
work I'd take the Métro from the Champs-Elysées and hang
out, sometimes till dawn, at the Monaco, the Bonaparte, Deux
Magots, Tabou, with Alfred, Elliott Stein, Ricardo Vigón, the
marvelous international stew of young expatriates that walked
the night from Montparnasse to St.-Germain and even to
Montmartre. Then, home to the hotel and bed till noon. A great
lunch/breakfast at Orestias or Chez Julien or the Beaux Arts and
then the terrasses de café – Old Navy, Select, Dôme – until five-
thirty and time to return to the rue de Berri for my night's work.[33]

This was the life into which Susan was initiated. Just as it was
Harriet who had emancipated Susan at Berkeley nearly a decade
before, it was Harriet who now freed her even further from her
marriage. Susan was surprised at Harriet's beauty now – she
had not thought of her as all that pretty before. But much as the
turbulent relationship between Susan and Harriet in 1958 was
once again liberating, it was also excruciatingly painful for Susan.
Harriet was still extricating herself from her long affair with Fornés
and her attraction to Susan was rather ambivalent, despite her
willingness to sleep with her. Susan was both less and more
attached to her previous relationship.

On 6 January 1958, Susan and Harriet took a room in the
Hôtel de l'Univers for nine days. Susan revelled in their reunion,
yet Harriet seemed distant, bored, edgy at times, and Susan was
tormented by anxious jealousies waiting up for her some nights.
Both women were keeping journals at this time: one of the more
painful episodes early in their affair was when Susan had read
some of the caustic remarks about herself in Harriet's diary. And

indeed, Harriet's diary reveals her lack of attraction to Susan, despite her awareness of how attractive she is: 'I've never before lived with someone I neither desired sexually nor felt strongly about. It's so decadent! I feel terrible about it all – brooding depression – '.[34]

On 16 January, Susan's birthday, they moved to the Hôtel de Poitou, where Harriet had lived with Irene. Burdened with the ghost of Irene's presence, the relationship became heated, leaving Susan in absolute love-sickness and despair.[35] 'When I do, infrequently, make love to her, I am either drunk or totally incompetent or technical, brutal, and cold', Harriet wrote in her diary. 'It's hideous of me but what can I do? I am simply not attracted to her.'[36] Yet they moved into Sam Wolfenstein's apartment together, and planned some summer travels. Harriet, for all her scorn, was afraid of being alone; Susan abased herself, tried to please her.

Philip's torrent of letters, meanwhile, announced that he had been fired and was looking for work in New York. He still didn't know exactly what was happening, had not been 'officially' dropped by Sontag, deliberating over the end of the marriage during all her time away, yet there was a growing desperation in his missives. But despite Susan's pain with Harriet, the unsuitability and even misery of her new relationship, the thought of returning to her old life was impossible. Her letters to Philip began to fall off; she found herself averse even to reading his letters. When he wrote with news of an impending job at Berkeley, Susan was merely grateful that it would make the break easier.[37] But she couldn't ask to divorce by letter. She had to tell him in person. 'My letters had to be loving. I had to wait till I returned', she wrote.[38]

In April, Harriet and Susan went to Spain and Morocco together for two weeks, visiting Madrid, Seville, Cadiz and Tangier. In Madrid they saw Bosch paintings at the Prado and went shopping, Susan aware again of Irene's haunting presence as Harriet spoke Spanish. In Seville, which they reached after a tortuous third-class train ride – they travelled cheaply all that

Susan in Seville, 1958.

summer, hitch-hiking and staying in cheap pensions – they saw a bullfight, made love in the afternoon and heard processions of soldiers in the streets. Susan found Cadiz, where they walked along the sea wall, beautiful and sad.[39] They took a bus to Algeciras, eating crevettes on the quay, waiting for the boat to Tangier. In Morocco they stayed in a spacious room with dazzling views of the sea; they drank mint tea and listened to the Arab musicians in the Sultan's palace. Yet for Susan the trip was disappointing. They didn't quarrel, yet neither were they that intimate. In May, after more time together in Paris, they went to Germany, speeding past Dachau on the autobahn in a ride they hitched with a Dutchman; in Munich the ruins of war and the American soldiers on the streets made a great impression on Susan. They went on to Berlin, then to Hamburg to see their painter friend Reinhard, who had a crush on Susan.

Harriet was feeling eclipsed by Susan's beauty which, she remarked, was noticed by everyone else that summer.[40] In July they travelled to Greece, seeing bouzouki dancers in the taverna gardens of Athens, visiting the Acropolis and staying in a hotel on a busy market in Evripidou Street which they eventually realized was a brothel.[41] They were arguing again, but continued to the island of Hydra. In Delphi, Susan noted the beauty of the mountains and cliffs, the sea, the pine trees with their fresh smell, the heat of the sun, the vibrating haze of the silver-green olive trees staggered along the hillside terraces. She was in love with the romance of travel, and would remain so; that summer a pattern of travel was set which Susan would repeat many times throughout her life – of spending long, suspended periods in Paris and Europe before (always) returning to New York. In Greece that summer, she knew her relationship with Harriet had a limited future, as she wrote of how all the beauty showed her she could get by without Harriet after all.[42] She left Greece, and Harriet, in August.

Yet this did not mean a return to Philip by any means. As Susan wrote years later, in the preface to her novel *In America*, it took her only ten days to get married, but almost as many years to build up the courage to think she had the moral right to divorce.[43] 'I lost a decade', she would sometimes later say, referring to the 1950s and her marriage with Rieff.[44] She would also say that she hadn't lived her life in the right order: her adult life came before her adolescence.[45] She had helped – more than helped – write a book, she had begun a thesis and had reams of notes in her diaries, but in the eyes of the world was not a writer at all. She was still half-formed. When Sontag returned to America, and to her son, towards the end of 1958, she was picked up on arrival in her home country by Philip, and she immediately told him it was over.

3

New York! New York! 1959–1965

Sontag moved to New York at the beginning of 1959, without Philip, but with David. She was determined to be independent, to make another clean break from the past. She had to find somewhere to stay and a way to support herself: she refused alimony from Philip, even though her lawyer advised her that she was entitled to it. She had to adjust to the city quickly. After Oxford, Paris, Spain and Greece, its lack of beauty was almost aggressive. She noted how ugly the city was in her diary soon after arrival, with David, very little money, and her divorce case pending. 'But I like it here, even like *Commentary*' – the journal where she found work as an editor in her first six months in New York.[1] She took a two-room apartment on 350 West End Avenue, which she furnished cheaply, visiting thrift stores.[2] David, then six, remembers this period as one of 'impecunious promise, discomfort, and enchantment'.[3] Susan would likewise see it in fairy-tale, dramatic terms: 'I was thrilled. I was like Irina in *The Three Sisters* longing for Moscow. All I could think was New York! New York!'[4]

The combination of the beckoning city and the freedom from her previous, heterosexual life at Harvard was intoxicating. 'Like smoke evaporating, my failed marriage wasn't there anymore', she wrote in her diary of this time; 'And my unhappy childhood slipped away also, as though touched by magic.'[5] Philip's reaction to the divorce was, as Susan had known it would be, cataclysmic. She had written in her diary that the blow would mark him for life.

Still, she did it. For a time, David shuttled between his mother in New York and his father in Stanford, where he stayed with Philip during the summers. Sontag's real family, and part of the family she had begun, were now both in California.

Breaking with Philip gave her, in reaction, a great momentum. She rebelled against his example as she sought to begin her own life as a writer. But she had absorbed his rigour and his academic training, which she would use, loosen and unfix throughout the 1960s; as she later realized, she always took something, creatively, from her relationships. Her dissertation was dropped, quietly, although periodically throughout the next decade she thought about finishing it. However, she did set about finding academic teaching positions in New York, beginning as an instructor in philosophy at Sarah Lawrence College and City College in the autumn of 1959. The following year Sontag started teaching a course in the sociology of religion at Columbia with her old friends Jacob and Susan Taubes.

Susan also met María Irene Fornés during her first year in New York, and the two became a couple, eventually ousting Harriet from both her former lovers' lives, although this was a gradual, inevitably messy process. Seeing Irene in New York, after Susan's Parisian months spent so uncomfortably in her shadow, must have been strange. Susan might very reasonably have resented Irene before she met her. But the opposite happened: attraction. Harriet returned to New York in the summer of 1959, staying for a while with Susan, who held a welcome-home party for her at which Harriet got so drunk she slipped, dancing, and broke her nose.[6] But by the end of the year, Irene was firmly installed in Susan's diaries as Harriet's successor. There was some irony – and victory – in Susan moving away from Harriet in this way, given that Harriet had throughout the previous year seen herself as merely tolerating Susan, whom she didn't really love. The split came abruptly, when Harriet went to Susan's apartment one day to find she was not there – Susan was with Irene, at Irene's flat. Irene spoke to Harriet on the phone, and told her she was now with Susan.[7] In her diary, Susan criticized herself for getting Irene to make this call, while she went to another room.[8]

While Harriet had been a liberating force for Sontag, years before in Berkeley and then in Paris, what Susan sought from Irene was more of a marriage. She was jealous whenever Irene spent time with someone else, and she was fiercely demanding, possessive of her.[9] Later, Susan wrote that Harriet had been a 'trial run' for her 'new being', while Irene had truly changed her, initiated her.[10] Desire between Susan and Irene was more equally matched than between Susan and Harriet.

Irene would also become a writer. She was petite, with short, dark curly hair, lively brown eyes and a beguilingly innocent expression which often hid her vociferous, passionate nature. Born in Havana in 1930, she had come to New York from Cuba with her mother after her father's death in 1945. She initially wanted to be a painter, travelling to France in the mid-1950s before switching to writing plays, being inspired by Roger Blin's original production of Beckett's *En attendant Godot* while in Paris. (This, she said, despite the fact that she knew no French.) On her return to America after Europe, Irene worked as a textile designer before she wrote her first plays, inspired as much by Susan as Susan was also inspired by her to try fiction. Writing formed a central part of their relationship. Irene, more profoundly than Harriet, loosened Susan up sexually – and Susan later thought she would never have been able to write fiction if this had not happened, severing the influence of Philip. They sometimes wrote in the same room. The poet Edward Field reports that Irene had told him that she and Susan used to sit 'across a table from each other, each at their typewriters, stopping to read to the other a passage they were proud of'.[11] Irene's first published play, *The Widow*, appeared in 1961, followed two years later by *There! You*

Al Carmines, María Irene Fornés, Harry Koutoukas and Larry Kornfield at a table in Caffe Cino in the West Village, *c.* 1966–7.

Died, beginning her long career in avant-garde theatre as a writer and director.

With Irene, Susan also began spending time in New York with the writer Alfred Chester. Alfred, flamboyantly gay, had been a confidante during the ups and downs of Harriet and Irene's relationship in Paris, where he had lived, after early years in Brooklyn, since 1951. A childlike vulnerability in Alfred was offset by a campy worldliness and appetite for flagrant gossip. He had always seen himself as an outsider, partly due to a childhood sickness which made him lose all his hair at seven, including his eyebrows and eyelashes. Cynthia Ozick, who first met Chester in composition classes at NYU in 1946, provides a memorable, semi-fictional portrayal of his physical appearance: 'Alfred, this fellow from Brooklyn, bleached-out eyes nearly yellow, no lashes, bald as an apple, the squat middle

of him round as Humpty Dumpty, short fluttery taffylike
fingers, a yellow wig (no exaggeration!) wobbling on his
shiny pate. Alfred knew them all, George Plimpton and
Jimmy Baldwin and the rest of them . . .'.[12] Chester was deeply
affected by the loss of his hair, and the wig, reported by others
as being orange, or orange-yellow, was outré and comically
ill-fitting, a source of lifelong embarrassment and ambiguous
shame. Until the wig was accidentally burned in a kitchen
accident in the 1960s and Alfred went out without it in public

Alfred Chester with editors of the *Paris Review* and *Merlin* outside the Café de
Tournon, *c.* 1954–5. Alfred is in the middle row, second from right, wearing glasses
and a scarf.

for the first time, the unavoidably noticeable, bizarre hairpiece was off-limits conversationally.[13]

Chester's early years in Paris held great promise, as he struck up literary contacts with the *Paris Review*, *Merlin*, edited by Alexander Trocchi, and the Princess Marguerite Caetani's *Botteghe Oscure*. He published a collection of short stories, *Here Be Dragons*, in 1955, and his first novel, *Jamie Is My Heart's Desire*, in 1956.[14] In her memoir 'Alfred Chester's Wig' (1992), a mischievous blend of praise and critique, Ozick writes that 'Chester's Paris stories were exquisite; focussed and given over to high diction, they seemed the work of an old hand. They had the tone and weight of translations from this or that renowned classical European author whose name you could not quite put your finger on: Colette, or Gide, or the author of "Death in Venice".'[15] Ozick was in awe of him; she even envied him.

Chester returned from Europe to New York at the end of the 1950s after a spell of several months on the Greek island of Salamis, fictionalized in his *New Yorker* story 'A War on Salamis', which funded his return to America. Susan looked up to Alfred: he was one of the first successful writers she knew. He was a few years older than her, born in 1928; his father, Jake, like her father Jack, had also been a Jewish immigrant to America from Europe, and also worked in the fur trade. Something in Alfred's demeanour and being, as Diana Athill recalls in her memoir *Stet* (2000), made absolute honesty possible when talking to him. Meeting Alfred when André Deutsch, for whom Athill worked as an editor, was publishing *Jamie Is My Heart's Desire* in England in 1956, Athill felt 'an instant recognition that with this person nothing need be hidden . . . (though there was a small dark pit of secrecy in the middle of the openness: I would never have spoken to him about his wig)'.[16] Susan felt this, too, for by 1960 she was remarking in her diary about her own tendency to be indiscreet and to show off – which she calls 'X' in the diaries – noting that Alfred shared this tendency.[17]

On his return to New York, Alfred, eternally penniless and adept at artful deceptions, had connived his way into a Greenwich Village apartment with a roof garden on Sullivan Street. Putting aside work on his unfinished novel, *I, Etc.*,[18] Chester began a prolific stint as a fearless critic and reviewer, for many of the journals that Susan would soon start to write for: *Commentary*, *Partisan Review*, the *New York Herald Tribune Book Week* and the *New York Review of Books*. Many of his most celebrated reviews were mercilessly witty demolition jobs, written at high pressure, through draft after draft, on Dexamyl, an amphetamine-barbiturate.[19] (Susan used Dexamyl too, for many years, from the 1960s apparently until the early '80s, as a stimulant for writing.[20])

Chester's reviews rapidly earned him notoriety. Chester for his part avowed that he wrote criticism only for the money, and longed to return to fiction. Susan, in her criticism, would never write the kind of acid, damning put-downs in which Alfred excelled: her role as a critic, when writing on individual works or authors, tended more towards a form of revelatory explication and ardent admiration, and when tackling wider cultural issues, a highly ambitious identification and diagnosis of broad themes. Yet Alfred, during these high-powered years in New York, was one of the first examples of a working critic Susan had seen at such close quarters, and he helped open up the world of New York reviewing to her.

Early in 1960, Susan and Irene were confiding in Alfred frequently. They told him of their complaints, their squabbles and their makings-up; they went out to restaurants with him, sometimes taking David too, and to parties. Despite David's youth, Sontag made the most of being in New York, going out frequently, very often to the Museum of Modern Art and the cinema, where she almost seemed to live some days. As in Paris, Susan went devotedly, almost religiously, to the movies. She always sat in the centre of the third row, a lifelong habit, so as to be overwhelmed by the image.[21] She saw dozens of films a month: sometimes her diaries simply turn into lists of films she has seen, as she absorbed the foreign movies being shown in New York at the Fifty-fifth Street Playhouse and Dan Talbot's New Yorker Theater.[22]

In her teaching at Columbia with Jacob and Susan Taubes, Sontag's course took in classes on religion and myth in China, Japan and India, as well as the Old Testament; meanwhile at Sarah Lawrence, she frequently arrived later than she should, occasionally missed classes and lectures, and felt bad about it.[23] She was, simultaneously, publishing her first critical articles and reviews, on various subjects including Freud and Antonioni (on the latter under the pseudonym 'Calvin Koff'). Her multifarious interests intersected, not always in obvious ways. Phillip Lopate, an under-graduate at Columbia from 1960 to 1964, remembers fondly the anecdotes of friends who attended Sontag's Introduction to Religion course, and how she told them to go to a Roberto Rossellini retrospective at MOMA.[24]

In 1960, Sontag also began writing 'Confessions of Hippolyte', or 'Dreams of Hippolyte', which became her first novel, *The Benefactor*. Sontag later said she wrote the novel at weekends and over two summers while she was teaching; as she told it, she wrote the first lines one evening after a conversation in a Greenwich Village coffeehouse, the Figaro, with a friend.[25] The novel was largely written during the summer of 1960, when Sontag spent three months in Cuba with Irene, and the summer of 1961, when the couple went to Europe, visiting Paris, Athens and Hydra, mirroring the itinerary Sontag mapped out with Harriet three years earlier. By this time, Sontag had a contract from Farrar, Straus & Giroux for the novel, based on its early chapters, which had impressed the publishers Robert Giroux and Roger Straus. By the early months of 1962, *The Benefactor* was finished.[26]

Sontag's novel set her apart from the realist tradition of many of her American contemporaries. In her diaries from around the time she began *The Benefactor*, as though thinking through what kind of fiction writer to be, Sontag listed several other writers – Saul Bellow, Ralph Ellison, Bernard Malamud, Philip Roth – all, she noted, grappling with everyday American experience.[27] She was not going to write like any of these figures. Her attraction was to an international canon, of which Samuel Beckett, Jorge Luis Borges, Franz Kafka and Vladimir Nabokov were exemplars. Her rejection of contemporary American writing was in tune with her rejection of so much contemporary American life, which had to do with her upbringing, her family and her sexuality. With *The Benefactor*, Sontag set out her stall with a hybrid of European traditions and American Surrealism – continuing the line of Poe, Djuna Barnes and Nathanael West. Drawing from her work on Freud and her teaching of philosophy, myth and religion, *The Benefactor* was concerned not so much with waking life but with the alogic of dreams and the 'dark half' of the mind.[28] In *Freud: The Mind of the Moralist*, Sontag and Rieff wrote that 'the interest of Poe, Baudelaire, Rimbaud, Nietzsche, is all in what Browning called "the dangerous edge of things"' – and this shadowy, visionary territory was very much that of *The Benefactor*, which opens with epigrams from De Quincey and Baudelaire on the irresponsibility of dreams, and with a nod to Descartes, '*je rêve donc je suis*' (I dream, therefore I am).[29]

Sontag later noted in her diaries that *The Benefactor* was an extreme exploration of 'solipsistic consciousness' and aestheticism, influenced by Baudelaire's portrayal of the dandy in *Mon coeur mis à nu* ('My Heart Laid Bare').[30] The dandy, Baudelaire wrote, should aspire to uninterrupted sublimity; he should live and sleep in front of a mirror. The narrator of *The Benefactor*, Hippolyte, a wealthy aesthete in his sixties now looking back on his life, does something similarly decadent, self-regarding and strange. His life project, as recounted in the novel, has been to understand his dreams, collect his dreams, eventually to live his dreams. He has tried to become a professional dreamer. The novel is a fictional memoir, an imaginary *Interpretation of Dreams*, an index of the unconscious, in which Hippolyte recounts his dream life in prose that is arch, epigrammatic, essayistic, deliberately archaic and dryly amusing. Hippolyte tells us of other titles he considered for his story, listed in his notebook – '*My Curious Dreams, Poor Hippolyte . . . The Confessions of a Self-Addicted Man, Notes of a Dreamer on His Craft*' – all of which make the aims of the novel clearer than *The Benefactor*.[31] Like James Joyce's *Finnegans Wake*, or the enigmatic paintings of Salvador Dalí, Max Ernst and René Magritte, the novel puts the dream life under the spotlight.

Hippolyte sets out on his quest in search of self-transcendence and fulfilment. 'I was not looking for my dreams to interpret my life, but rather for my life to interpret my dreams', he writes.[32] Dreams, the unconscious, the irrational, nightly half of existence should not be impatiently swept aside by reason when the day resumes, Hippolyte's project suggests, but thought about, even acted on. 'All dreams are model *self-analyses*', Sontag wrote in her diaries: the better the dream, the harder to decipher.[33] In attempting to comprehend the movements of his dream life, Hippolyte tries to understand something about his essential self.

The setting of *The Benefactor*, which, as Ozick noted tartly of Alfred Chester's Paris stories, sometimes feels as though it were translated from a forgotten classic European text, is Paris in the early twentieth century. Specifics are deliberately eluded or blurred, however, creating a hallucinatory, timeless, placeless feel. Hippolyte's waking life and dream life form the two alternating narrative strands of the novel, reflecting and intersecting with each other. In his dream life, Hippolyte finds himself in various surreal situations. In his first dream he is trapped in a narrow room, forced to dance to a flute and chained to the wall by a woman he desires. In his second dream, he enters a party where the guests play a game of bending over in a 'U' shape to the floor – which he wins.

Both these dreams, Hippolyte decides, are sexual in origin. His third dream is religious: he enters a church where, seated in an electric chair, he soars higher and higher.

In his waking life, Hippolyte meets with a friend, Jean-Jacques, a writer and ex-boxer who spends his days writing and his nights as a gay prostitute, in another play on the usual roles of waking and sleeping. Hippolyte accompanies Jean-Jacques on his nocturnal adventures and even sleeps with him once; the main focus of Hippolyte's daylight hours, however, falls on the seduction of an aristocratic woman, Frau Anders, into whose salon he gains admission after publishing his only piece of writing: a philosophical article proposing 'important ideas on a topic of no great importance'.[34]

Hippolyte's dream life and his waking life are relatively distinct at the outset of *The Benefactor*, but they start to merge as Hippolyte's 'waking' behaviour becomes increasingly whimsical. He travels with Frau Anders to an Arab city, and sells her into slavery. He seduces Frau Anders's daughter Lucrezia ('I was not unaware that there was something unseemly in my inheriting the daughter after enjoying the mother').[35] He enters 'the temple of public dreams, the cinema', by becoming an actor in the first decade of sound films for a Scandinavian director.[36] He sees Frau Anders on her return from the Arab city and finds her horribly mutilated; he attempts to burn down her house and murder her, though whether he is successful in this remains unclear. Receiving an inheritance on his father's death, Hippolyte decorates a town house for Frau Anders, or her ghostly double, to live in, while he marries an officer's daughter, who dies from leukaemia. It appears towards the end that Hippolyte has gone mad, has lost all sense of reality; he cannot tell where his dreams end and his real life begins. Sontag taunts us at the close with hints that we have been reading the narrative the wrong way round: that what we might have taken as Hippolyte's waking life was his dream life, and vice versa.

The Benefactor is a riddle. It invites and provokes interpretation from the reader, just as all dreams do, while it remains constantly indecipherable. The novel, Sontag said, has 'systematically obscure elements'.[37] It is also ingeniously asymmetrical in design. 'I have found that there are symmetrical ideas and asymmetrical ones as well', Hippolyte writes. 'The ideas which interest me are asymmetrical: one enters through one side and exits through a side which is shaped quite differently.'[38] One enters and exits Hippolyte's story in a similarly curious way as one reads it, as one calibrates and recalibrates its balance between dreams and reality.

Hippolyte's project of self-discovery and self-realization through his dreams is presented as admirable and ridiculous in equal measure. His search for a reconciliation of desires and realities – above all, of sexual desires and realities – echoes *Freud*, in which Sontag and Rieff wrote that 'the highest and healthiest freedom is, then, not to deny the emotions, the unconscious life, but – knowingly – to enact their demands.'[39] Yet while Hippolyte's quixotic search for his ultimate self undeniably appeals to Sontag, she has fun mocking his self-absorption. In a diary entry written after seeing the experimental theatre director Jerzy Grotowski at work, Sontag wrote that Grotowski had put the ideas about self-transcendence in *The Benefactor* into practice. While Sontag distanced herself from these ideas through a sustained irony, Grotowski was in earnest.[40]

One of the pleasures of *The Benefactor* is Hippolyte's voice, and his aphoristic turns of phrase. As a novelist, Sontag often wrote as though she was writing non-fiction. Hippolyte has all the intelligence of his creator, and his startling aperçus are inserted smoothly into the narrative flow which, exploiting the memoir form, is capacious enough for digression. Hippolyte is especially essayistic and loquacious on the nature and peculiarities of dreams, the anarchy of the unconscious. He muses at length, almost as if writing a long essay 'on dreams'.

The Benefactor offers an extended analogy of the writing life, its potential and its dangers. 'What if the life on which the dreams fed withered, and the dreams flourished?', asks Hippolyte – exactly, one might say, over time, the relation between writers and their work.[41] Sontag was fascinated with the notion of writing as professional dreaming, and the oscillations between art and life, which like dreams and life also become interrelated. She wanted her life to benefit from her work, not just her work from her life. Clearly Sontag relished inhabiting Hippolyte's aristocratic, dandyish voice, and she did so with panache. But after *The Benefactor*'s self-absorption, Sontag's own trajectory as a writer would begin to move outwards: towards a willed effort to 'pay attention to the world'.[42] This balanced the almost religious self-investigation in Sontag's sense of her vocation, as much as her aestheticism, her love of sensual pleasure, her passion and voracity.

Her own writing life would be, like Hippolyte's, a constant chasing after dreams. And peculiarly, certain things in *The Benefactor* – the notoriety after writing a controversial article on 'a topic of no great importance', working with a Scandinavian film director, visiting an Arab city – would mirror her own life, prophetically. Yet the novel held its example before her of the weakness of outright aestheticism, of failing to register the impact of reality, and she always heeded this.

As she was finishing *The Benefactor* in 1962, Susan had begun seeing an analyst, Diana Kemeny, who focused her on understanding her past; like Hippolyte, she was 'crawling through the tunnel of myself' with Diana, and saw her throughout the 1960s.[43] Susan's relationship with Irene, however, was becoming turbulent. Even at the beginning of their love, Sontag confessed qualms about Irene to her diary, writing in 1960 that they were already weary of each other, not really talking properly anymore, and reflecting on how, with Philip, the real trouble started when they stopped making up after quarrels.[44] Sontag had already begun to gauge the limits of her new lover. She had done so almost from the start. This never took Sontag very long, this realization of the finite nature of others' capabilities; with it came a slowing of the early soaring bliss of her romances. And Susan and Irene quarrelled often.

One of Susan's complaints was over Irene's 'ceaseless emotional book-keeping'.[45] With Irene's imprecations, guilt and perpetual atonement crept in on Susan's side, an endless emotional debt to Irene she felt she could never repay. They tried separating for some periods, and Susan found that separation from Irene made her unhappy. Irene often stayed at Alfred's apartment, sometimes when he was away. She was always closer to Alfred than Susan was. Irene also spent some time in 1963 in Mexico on a *beca* (scholarship) from the Mexican government, inviting Alfred to do the same.[46] As Edward Field relates, Alfred bought an ageing Chevrolet and 'drove to Mexico . . . vaguely expecting to meet up with Fornés in Mexico City'.[47] But he ended up in Vera Cruz.

In April 1963, Susan's diary charts the build-up of tension with Irene. Chester, displaying his inveterate 'X'-y love of gossip, wrote to Edward Field that Susan and Irene were 'still lovers but seldom' that April, but by the end of that month, 'Susan and Irene ne sont plus. It officially ended yesterday.'[48] This was the close of their four-year affair and Susan, in her diaries later that year and for several years after, reeled with loneliness and pain. In August she wrote that she was afraid of being alone, without any reassurance or warmth; she felt anxious lying down, standing up, when taking a bath. She was clinging to David.

I'm afraid to take hold, afraid to let go
continual deceit > guilt > anxiety . . .
Do something
Do something
Do something[49]

The Benefactor came out in September 1963, to mixed but respectful reviews. Alfred had gone to Morocco where he would stay for the next few years after being urged to go out there by Paul Bowles, the two having met at a dinner party earlier that year in New York and begun an excited correspondence. Since finishing her novel, Sontag found it hard to start another long work of fiction, concentrating on becoming a critic. In one way this was her first reaction to the self-absorption of *The Benefactor*, showing her readiness to immerse herself in contemporariness, to turn outwards to other people, other arts. On the other hand, she might have felt she was settling for second best, for throughout her life Sontag always claimed she was primarily a writer of fiction, and berated herself for her incurable addiction to essay writing. Yet Sontag's lifelong oscillation between critical and creative writing was an intrinsic part of her gift; the two spheres nourished each other. Her criticism was all the more interesting because she was a novelist; her novels also drew from her essays. And Sontag was, from the start, a magisterial, brilliant essayist.

In the summer of 1962 Sontag achieved the dream of her adolescence, when her first ever piece for *Partisan Review* appeared: a review of a novel by Isaac Bashevis Singer. And the next year she was included in the newly launched *New York Review of Books*, writing on Simone Weil, a speciality of Susan Taubes, who wrote a thesis on Weil. A succession of other pieces for *PR* and the *NYRB* followed: on Nathalie Sarraute and the *nouveau roman*, Jean-Paul Sartre's *Saint Genet*, Albert Camus' *Notebooks*, Claude Lévi-Strauss' *Tristes Tropiques*, Michel Leiris' *L'Age d'homme*, and a series entitled 'Going to Theatre'. Sontag was also writing on film, producing essays on Alain Resnais' *Muriel* for *Film Quarterly*, Robert Bresson for *Seventh Art* and Jean-Luc Godard's *Vivre sa vie* for *Moviegoer*. Then, in autumn 1964, in *Partisan Review*, came 'Notes on "Camp"'.

Sontag was a distinctive critic for both what she wrote about and how she wrote about it. Just as in her life she was voracious in her appreciation of other arts, she wrote with equal interest, knowledge and passion on literature, theatre and film in her early essays. The register of her criticism was also poised between worlds, often touching the high rigour of an academic tone but also taking important freedoms which made the pieces personal, even if they seldom used the first person.[50]

Partly, this personal element came from the topics Sontag chose to write about in her essays, which were usually records of her enthusiasms and were not generally written to commission but selected by her, guided by her own interests. Sontag wrote many early reviews, but her favoured approach and form were not of the standard evaluative type. Nor, conversely, even in the early 1960s when Sontag was still at Columbia and Sarah Lawrence, did she ever bow down to academic conventions and trends; later, she had a careful way of being aware of the waves of French theory, structuralism and deconstruction of the late 1970s and '80s while retaining her own independent voice. Her film criticism, likewise, was mostly written before the advent of film theory.

When Sontag started publishing essays, another facet of her originality was her bold divergence from the New York Intellectuals of the period, a group that included Clement Greenberg, Irving Howe, Dwight Macdonald, William Phillips, Philip Rahv and Harold Rosenberg. This lay above all in the willingness and ease with which she moved between 'high' and 'low' culture, freely crossing boundary lines demarcated and fiercely defended by her predecessors. Sontag's radical style in her essays assisted in her redrawing of what it was possible to talk about critically, which soon redefined the terms of discussion for a generation. This style was aphoristic; sharp, swift, nimble; often unharnessed to quotation; imperially authoritative while whimsically provocative and capricious, even wilfully perverse; able to move suddenly between particular works and their ramifications in society; casually, off-handedly referential to a whole array of European traditions generally ignored by contemporary American critics.

Sontag's essays imported a fleet of mostly French writers, film-makers and thinkers into New York intellectual life, conveying their originality and appeal. At the same time, her criticism has a blistering scepticism and capacity for fine lines of reasoning. The essays offer breathtaking flights of daring, rhetoric and calculated opposition. Perhaps Sontag was so drawn to writing them because they satisfied both the ascetic and the aesthete within her, the writer and the reader, the moralist and the pleasure-seeker, the recluse and the performer. She collected the subjects of her essays, showed her discernment in discovering them, revelled in the acquisition of knowledge and access to other experience.

When she devoted herself to an essay, Sontag would intellectually devour her subject in a fierce, instinctive act of assessment and appropriation. She would wear her subject like a mask. The early essays came more easily than those in later decades – an essay of 1982 on Roland Barthes, 'Writing Itself', took her six months to write – but they still required dozens of drafts, with Sontag often changing her mind about a subject while writing about it.[51]

A selection of essays written between 1962 and 1965 became her second book, *Against Interpretation*, published early in 1966 and dedicated to Sontag's friend, the artist Paul Thek. Many of the pieces were significantly revised before the book's publication and were arranged in a sequence that gave them more coherence, above all by being framed by the title essay. This gave the collection a manifesto.

'Against Interpretation' rails against what Sontag saw as one of the prevailing trends of her era: the search for 'hidden' meanings. The germ of Sontag's mistrust of interpretation had its roots in her study of Freud but the same malaise, she thought, afflicted literary criticism too. What Sontag urged – if there was to be criticism at all – was a sensuous approach to form and style,

as opposed to the presumptuous excavation of 'meaning'
which was, in an age 'based on excess, on overproduction',
stifling, obfuscating, occluding.[52] 'We must learn to *see* more,
to *hear* more, to *feel* more', Sontag wrote.[53] The function of
criticism was to achieve a vital apprehension of art and life
as it is, rather than add to the reduplicating shadow worlds
of hermeneutics.

'Against Interpretation' veers close to promoting a critical
muteness, which either wanted criticism to become more than
it ever could be, or to say nothing at all. It is a quixotic, self-
contradictory title for a volume of critical essays, which while
startlingly tight and fresh in its focus does not exactly refrain from
analysis. And indeed the title was a tease, slightly ironic, since
Sontag knew that for a critic to be utterly 'against interpretation'
was an impossibility. But it was an important gesture of defiance
to the prevailing critical habits of the early 1960s.

The broad appeal of *Against Interpretation* lies in its diversity, as
Sontag writes on different art forms, making connections between
them; the collection also gains from the underlying sense that
Sontag was prospecting in the worlds of anthropology, literary
criticism, philosophy, the *nouveau roman*, the theatre and cinema
to forge her own novelistic aesthetic as well as a new way of seeing
the world. There is very little in *Against Interpretation* on fiction or
the novel, as even the essays on literature tend towards life-writing,
philosophy or other criticism. But some pieces did serve as justifi-
cations and explanations of Sontag's own work as a novelist. The
only essay on contemporary art, 'Happenings: An Art of Radical
Juxtaposition', described events staged in the early 1960s by
Allan Kaprow, Jim Dine, Carolee Schneemann and others in New
York, relating them to a broad tradition of Surrealism central to
The Benefactor, many of whose dream sequences recall Sontag's
descriptions of happenings, which she attended throughout her
first years in New York, having met the artist Claes Oldenburg a

few weeks after arriving in the city.[54] The essay allowed Sontag to obliquely explain and position her own novel.

> By Surrealism, I do not mean a specific movement in painting inaugurated by André Breton's manifesto in 1924 and to which we associate the names of Max Ernst, Dali, Chirico, Magritte, and others. I mean a mode of sensibility which cuts across all the arts in the 20th century . . . united by the idea of destroying conventional meanings, and creating new meanings or counter-meanings through radical juxtaposition . . . if the meaning of modern art is its discovery beneath the logic of everyday life of the alogic of dreams, then we may expect the art which has the freedom of dreaming also to have its emotional range. There are witty dreams, solemn dreams, and there are nightmares.[55]

Sontag's interest in Surrealism as a continuing sensibility of 'radical juxtaposition' also explained her fascination during the 1960s with William Burroughs, whose 'cut-up' method likewise worked as an art of startling, sometimes nightmarish splicing and grew, from a different angle, out of a similar tradition. Sontag claimed that Burroughs, with his freedom from realism, was the American writer who interested her most when she wrote *Against Interpretation*, and an essay on the heroin-addicted Beat, 'William Burroughs and the Novel', appeared in the German and French editions of *Against Interpretation*, but not in the English.[56]

'Notes on "Camp"' takes Sontag's interest in Surrealism in more playful directions. 'Many things in the world have not been named; and many things, even if they have been named, have never been described', the essay begins. One of these things is 'the sensibility . . . that goes by the cult name of "Camp"'. The following 'notes', 'for' Oscar Wilde, were written, like Sontag's diaries, not in consecutive prose but in 'the form of jottings'.[57] Into the dazzlingly over-wrought, indeed slightly camp display of erudition which followed, identifying camp in 'movies, clothes, furniture, popular songs, novels, people, buildings',[58] Sontag poured all her experience, mounting her most sustained affront to the New York Intellectuals's critical gate-keeping and showing how her essays, as much as her fiction, were an art of 'radical juxtaposition'.

Dissolving at points into one of Sontag's favourite literary forms, the list, 'Notes on "Camp"' ranges across points high- and low-brow, operatic and trashy, gay and straight, succeeding in its accumulations in rewiring them as it moves across Art Nouveau, *Swan Lake*, Luchino Visconti, *King Kong*, Ronald Firbank, Ivy Compton-Burnett, Jean Cocteau, André Gide, Greta Garbo, Warner Brothers musicals, Alfred Hitchcock, *Ivan the Terrible I* and *II*, William Blake and Japanese science fiction films, suggesting how all of them are, and are not, demonstrative of the elusive, so-bad-it's-good quality of camp. The deliriously referential pages of 'Notes on "Camp"' also invoke the figure of the dandy, so formative to Sontag's conception of Hippolyte in *The Benefactor*:

> The dandy was overbred. His posture was disdain, or else *ennui*. He sought rare sensations, undefiled by mass appreciation. (Models: Des Esseintes in Huysmans' *A Rebours*, *Marius the Epicurean*, Valéry's *Monsieur Teste*.) He was dedicated to 'good taste' . . . Camp – Dandyism in the age of mass culture – makes no distinction between the unique object and the mass-produced object. Camp taste transcends the nausea of the replica . . . Where the dandy would be continually offended or bored, the connoisseur of Camp is continually amused, delighted.[59]

'Notes on "Camp"' pointed the way towards the levelling of aesthetic styles and values in postmodernism, throwing the doors wide open. Appropriately, given its concerns with mass reproduction – and despite its initial appearance in *Partisan Review*, with its relatively small, elite circulation – it was a roaring success, making Sontag, suddenly, into an intellectual celebrity, the 'Queen of Camp'. The piece was mentioned at some length in *Time* and soon picked up by other reporters. This was gratifying for Sontag, still only just over 30 years old, but it also became unhelpful for her. And, while granting numerous interviews and tasting the glare of celebrity, she also stepped back from it and from the obvious paths she might have followed. While *Against Interpretation* displays an omnivorous love of 'high' and 'low' culture, Sontag's future essays would move steadily back to the high ground of late modernism, cultivating austerity, severity, seriousness. Ironically, it was the very success of 'Notes on "Camp"' that enabled Sontag to retreat from mass culture. She remained ambivalent about the essay, never writing on camp again and becoming irked when people asked her about it, as they would for the rest of her life.

In 1964 Sontag's status as an emerging underground star was confirmed when she visited Andy Warhol's Factory to sit for a series of his *Screen Tests*, the short, black-and-white silent films that Warhol made between 1964 and '66, for which he requested his subjects sit without blinking in front of a static camera. The *Screen Tests* stretched their subjects' ability to withstand the scrutiny of intense portraiture as much as their desire to improvise or project a certain pose, which usually broke down over the duration of the short film as the camera's mechanical gaze gave its microscopic revelations of personality. Sontag sat for seven *Screen Tests* for Warhol, which must have intrigued her as a future film-maker, and also offered a chance for the self-projection she had been willing herself towards for years in her diaries. Thirty-one, fresh-faced and youthful, Sontag runs through an array of expressions and actions in her *Screen Tests*, whose focus often blurs or bleaches into overexposure: coy, naive, sultry, distracted, restless, melancholic, smiling, resting her chin on her hand, laughing, shrugging, smoking, and in one, grinning manically, parodically, toothily, perhaps saying 'cheese'.[60]

Sontag left her position teaching religion at Columbia in 1964, and took up a more creative role as writer-in-residence at Rutgers. In the next two years a grant from the Rockefeller Foundation, and then a Guggenheim Fellowship, enabled Sontag to write full-time. This was the first time she had been able to do so, and she appreciated it. But she could not, at the same time, seem to get over her personal loneliness. In August 1964 she thought she should go away for a year in order to dispel her obsession with Irene, which she was not yet able to replace with another love. In London, she saw the writer and director Jonathan Miller, who became a long-standing friend and would interview her, talking about kitsch for almost an hour, on the BBC television series *Monitor*; then she was in Paris for the summer, avidly movie-going, still unhappy, licking her romantic wounds. The four years she had spent with Irene now seemed an impossibly long period, pressing down on her.[61] She felt wronged by Irene and knew she had to transpose this emotion, willing herself into action in her diary to transcend her passive suffering and misery. Her friendships, for instance with Paul Thek, did not fill the gap left by Irene; they were 'weightless'. She felt 'unattractive', 'unloveable', 'incomplete'.[62]

Glimmers of tranquillity appeared in May 1965 with a stay at Jasper Johns's house in Edisto Beach, South Carolina. David Rieff writes that Sontag had a relationship with Johns around this time; certainly they were good friends. Sontag found Johns intriguing for his reticence, his intellectual ideas about the autonomy of the artwork, his sense of everything as being 'interesting'. While staying with him, an aspiration she noted in her diaries under 'PROJECTS' – 'to see more' – got under way as she appreciated, noticed, noted nature more than usual, almost seeing everything as sculpture or as art.[63] Crucially, Jasper, or 'Jap', redirected and reoriented Susan's attention. Susan's relationship with Johns, and by extension, being brought into the orbit of Robert Rauschenberg and John Cage, would play a large part in the piece

A still from one of Andy Warhol's *Screen Tests* for Susan Sontag, 1964.

on 'The Aesthetics of Silence' collected in her next book of essays. At Edisto Beach, Sontag admired the thick, green, Spanish moss drooping from the trees; she luxuriated in the warmth and calm of the ocean and read Schoenberg's letters at midnight. She also began to develop ideas for a novel about an abstract artist, perhaps one devoted to a spiritual project.[64]

Sontag spent the summer of 1965 in Paris, once again, backtracking into resentment and anguish over Irene, as an exchange of letters with her ex-lover stirred up her feelings anew. Sontag wrote in her diary that Irene had been jealous of David, the one part of Susan's life that was hers alone. He was everything to her, especially now. Sontag wrote that if she hadn't had David, she would have committed suicide the previous year.[65] David, as he grew up, would inherit his mother's love of travel, as well as for writing: he would become a writer and editor (including of his mother's work, at Farrar, Straus & Giroux), specializing in reportage and humanitarian issues. Yet much as mother and son were inseparable, throughout David's childhood Susan also embarked on long travels. Her refusal of familial convention must have been liberating and, equally, difficult. David *was* everything to her, but she was also, undeniably, wedded to her work, which made great demands on them both. As David writes, Sontag

> oscillated between pride and regret over her sense of having sacrificed so much in the way of love and pleasure for her work or, as she almost invariably referred to it, *the* work . . . *The* work had to be served, and served at any price.[66]

Jasper Johns on the rooftop outside his studio apartment in New York, 1965.

Sontag's inability to get satisfactorily started on her next novel throughout this period was a great source of frustration to her. The diaries teem with ideas, but there were too many of them, coming from too many sources. Sontag was developing her interests in visual art, theatre and music, making lists of things to investigate and remember and of essays to write, and notes for essays which she did eventually publish. Her notebooks from 1965 overflow with references – to Cage, Duchamp, Francis Picabia, James Rosenquist, Buckminster Fuller and so many others – as well as lists of potential plots and scenarios.[67] The references to the visual arts, in particular, show her aggravation with the relatively retrograde nature of the novel. It was hard, she noted, to get people to see novels as abstract objects. People who instinctively under-stood the artworks of Larry Poons or Frank Stella, Sontag wrote, were baffled by the comparably abstract work of Gertrude Stein in literature.[68]

In her ideas notebook, however, Sontag had narrowed things down enough to develop an extended narrative called 'The Ordeal of Thomas Faulk', elements of which turned up in later works including *Death Kit* and Sontag's first film *Duet for Cannibals*, but which was finally abandoned.[69] The Faulk narrative was initially about the central character's breakdown, after his childhood in California and time in a boarding house, set mostly in a clinic in South Carolina, where Faulk went after his collapse. It appears to have been connected at first, however loosely, to the idea of the 'artist novel', which was further developed in conversations with Paul Thek at the all-night delicatessen Ratner's in Greenwich Village.[70] No doubt inspired by Thek's own work, particularly his faux-'organic' sculptures or 'technological reliquaries' such as *Meat Piece with Warhol Brillo Box* (1965) – in which a wax sculpture of raw meat was contained in a Warhol box – Sontag's 'artist novel' idea seems to have begun to turn around an artist who worked in wax. Over the next few years, perhaps because of

Susan and David at home in 1967.

Peter Hujar, *Paul Thek (11)*, 1975.

these conversations, Sontag and Thek worked almost in parallel on projects that explored similar concepts.

Towards the end of August 1965, Sontag was in Corsica, then Marseilles to take the boat to Tangiers. She had written a few months earlier to Alfred and to Paul Bowles, who had, cattily, compared each other's letters. Alfred had adjusted extremely quickly to Morocco, setting up with a young fisherman, Dris, whom, unbeknown to Alfred, had been groomed by Bowles to seduce Alfred.[71] Living at first in the small seaside town of Asilah with Dris, close to Bowles, Alfred had continued to write a monthly column for *Book Week* and other pieces for the New York press. His book of stories *Behold Goliath* had appeared to a disappointingly lukewarm reception in 1964, and he had written a surrealist novel, *The Exquisite Corpse*, for which he was trying to find a publisher. Susan had read it before she arrived in Tangiers.

As soon as she met Alfred, on arrival, she found him changed. Out of craziness, envy or drug-induced delusion, Alfred couldn't deal with Susan in Morocco, and made her feel unwelcome. The trip proved catastrophic – terminal – for their relationship. Susan saw straight away that there was something seriously wrong with Alfred, who despite being hypersensitive to drugs was self-medicating with Dexamyl, kief and, probably, LSD. Susan wrote in her diary that underneath all his contradictory layers of personality, Alfred had always been like a bad-tempered child. With his wig now gone, he talked incessantly to Susan about how hideous he had always felt. Had he ever been wise, Susan wondered, or had he just lost his wisdom? His hostility to Susan made her vow never again to be seduced, through lack of self-confidence, by the 'bullies': Harriet, Irene, Alfred. She felt stronger in herself now, paradoxically, as she knew she could withstand the worst. She was absolutely alone, and unloved – which had always been her greatest fear – yet she was still surviving.[72]

Alfred, meanwhile, was extremely paranoid: he wouldn't eat meals out in case he was poisoned; wouldn't even accept coffee from Dris; thought that the loss of his wig (which had caught fire while he was using the stove) had invalidated his passport. He broke Dris's watch, thinking there was a microphone inside it. He thought everything he was saying was being broadcast, that everyone was looking at him all the time, that he was being followed. He thought he was a hermaphrodite. Susan asked Dris how long Alfred had been like this – and also told Paul Bowles she believed Alfred was going genuinely mad. She was, sadly, right: Alfred had begun a steep descent that would culminate, in Jerusalem in 1971, with his death. Susan could see that no one

Alfred Chester and Dris in Morocco in the 1960s.

in Morocco would do the slightest thing about Alfred; perhaps she saw the pathos and the sadness of that situation. In Morocco, she wrote, people were looking to be radically '*dépaysé*', or disoriented; if you went crazy, others were mildly sympathetic but didn't really care.[73] Alfred was embroiled in a malicious, high-camp milieu which Susan previously thought only existed in the novels of Firbank or Jane Bowles.

In Morocco, Sontag met the Bowleses, and talked with Burroughs's friend Alan Ansen about 'cut-ups', dream machines, *The Soft Machine* and the comic 'routines' in *Naked Lunch*. She took a cab to nearby Tétouan with Ira and Rosalind Cohen, where she walked in the gardens in the Spanish quarter. She took kief.[74] She heard the cocks crow at dawn just outside the city every morning; visited Dris's brother Hamid, in hospital with a gangrenous foot; compiled lists of Alfred's sayings. She was preparing to leave, to return to America and David in September. But her trip to Morocco had done something profound to her psyche. In Tangier, Sontag felt she had entered Charenton, the insane asylum where the

Marquis de Sade had been held outside Paris in the late eighteenth and early nineteenth centuries. She herself had never been as thoroughly disoriented, alienated and entranced, she wrote in her diary, since her life-changing weekend in San Francisco with Harriet in 1949.[75]

4

Styles of Radical Will, 1966–1968

After so many false starts, Sontag began her second novel, *Death Kit*, in New York towards the end of 1965. Faint trails of the abandoned fictions she had been working on inevitably clung to the novel, but she saw *Death Kit* as an entirely fresh attempt. Her early novels had their genesis in a specific visionary moment, and tended to come in a flash, all at once, entire, intact – which was a source of mystery and wonderment to her even years later. *Death Kit*, as Susan told it to friends and lovers, began in a conversation she had that autumn, on a midnight coffee date with the poet John Hollander at the Tant Mieux, a late-night café on Bleecker Street. Hollander mentioned in passing the nickname 'Diddy', which their friend Richard Howard, the translator, poet and critic, had growing up in Cleveland.[1] The word magically unlocked the plot of a novel in Sontag's mind, as Hollander talked. Sontag asked to be excused, saying she had to take a long-distance phone call – an amusing unconscious metaphor for beginning a novel. She rushed home at 12.30 and wrote the long first section of *Death Kit*, staying up until six in the morning. By the middle of November, she knew roughly how long the book was going to take, as she wanted to have completed a first draft by January, writing five pages a day for 60 days.[2]

What was it about the name 'Diddy' that had such creative resonance? Sontag didn't know until several years later, in 1972, when one day she suddenly realized. 'Diddy, Daddy.' She expanded on this in her diary. Diddy, the central character in *Death Kit*, is 33 years old when he dies (and Susan turned 33 while writing *Death Kit*); her father was also 33 when he died, and failed to come home from China. 'Did-he? Did he die?' Susan now recognized the motif of 'false death' running through all her work up to that time – it was also there in the half-death of Frau Anders in *The Benefactor*, and would reappear in her films – rooted in her own uncertainty over her father's death. The realization of this inspiration for Diddy in *Death Kit*, as Susan wrote in 1972, brought her to an acceptance of what happened. 'It's finished. Daddy did die.'[3] At 39, she could write that, understand it, and close the door, she thought. But in *Death Kit*, the door between life and death remains half-open.

The title *Death Kit*, and the novel's dedication to Sontag's analyst Diana Kemeny, who shared the initials D. K., points to the influence of Sontag's psychoanalysis on her second long work of fiction, which continued the Freudian and Surrealist inheritance of *The Benefactor*, being likewise full of dreams and sub-narratives whose 'real' occurrence was less than probable in waking life, emanating instead from the febrile, unconscious self. *Death Kit* also furthered Sontag's exploration of ideas about religion and myth from her teaching, and led her again into the fantastic territory of Kafka, Burroughs and Borges. It particularly resembled Borges's short story 'The South'. In the Borges story, the main character is injured while walking up some stairs with a German translation of the *Thousand and One Nights* in his hands. Infected with blood poisoning, he enters a sanatorium or 'suburb of hell'. After leaving the hospital, he takes a train south, and has a series of adventures which end in a knife fight. However, everything that occurs in this story after his first entry into the 'suburb of hell' can also, as Borges intended, be read as purely mental elaborations that occur as he lies dying in the sanatorium.

In *Death Kit*, Sontag mines a similar idea with Diddy. Where *The Benefactor* recounted scores of dreams, and contrasted the dream world with the waking world, however invertedly or interrelatedly,

the entire fabric of *Death Kit* seemingly belongs to one extended
dream or hallucination, as the narrative takes place between
Diddy's suicide and his actual death. The text is Diddy's death
dream, occurring while he is at death's door, in a coma after
swallowing an overdose of sleeping pills. Sontag keeps the reader
in some suspense throughout as to whether Diddy is alive or dead,
and exploits this ambiguity.

Death Kit can thus be read in two different ways: as a work
of improbable but just about feasible realism, in which Diddy
did not die from his overdose of sleeping pills at the opening; and
as an extended dream fable recounting the flow of Diddy's dying
consciousness in his final post-overdose delirium, barely aware
of the world outside his mind. The two-way design is ingenious,
but in some ways backfired because of its own ingenuity. Many
reviewers and critics failed to see that *Death Kit* takes place in
a coma, judging it instead a work of insufficiently real realism,
a narrative off-centred not deliberately, but because of Sontag's
inability to craft a credible realist novel.[4] As in *The Benefactor*,
Sontag favoured the novelistic riddle which outwits interpretation;
once again, this was a high-risk and entirely conscious strategy.

One of Sontag's pointers as to what is going on in *Death Kit* is
the word '(now)', placed in brackets at various moments in the text,
obtrusively puncturing straight realism. Among other readings, this
device can be said to mark real time passing distortedly, unevenly,
in the world outside Diddy's mind as he dies. It is not clear whether
the entire narrative of *Death Kit* takes place over seconds, minutes,
hours or days, but one possibility is that each '(now)' sometimes
marks a mere second. Elsewhere, influenced by Burroughs's
Naked Lunch, Sontag shifts between third-person narration, which
introduces Diddy in conventional realist terms – 'Dalton Harron,
in full: a mild fellow, gently reared in a middle-sized city in
Pennsylvania' – and occasional references to 'we', suggesting
the story is being experienced and narrated by Diddy himself.[5]

While searching for a subject for a novel, Sontag had written that she was not looking for a plot so much as a '"tone"' or '"colour"'; often, she allowed the stirrings of voice alone, rather than plot or theme, to help her begin a narrative.[6] The palette in *Death Kit* is gruesomely grey, in keeping with the melancholy tendencies of someone who, as David Rieff tells us, kept a skull on a shelf behind her desk for decades as a memento mori.[7] 'Diddy, not really alive, had a life', Sontag declares early on, introducing the half-existence of her suicidal central figure, who never achieved self-possession. At the opening of *Death Kit*, everything is running down, liquefying, distorting, already nearly terminal; Diddy's monologue is an ooze, a dribble of words, probably never escaping his comatose skull. Like a Francis Bacon figure, Diddy's

> words like acrid chalk-coloured cubes spill out of a rotating cage . . . Diddy gasps for breath and, wherever he moves, bruises himself . . . Diddy, a failed amphibian. For whom all tasks have become senseless, all space inhospitable, virtually all people grotesque, all climates unseasonable, and all situations dangerous.[8]

Swallowing half a bottle of sleeping pills, he enters 'some dark time, in which it's hard to breathe', falls out of bed, hears his dog Xan barking, is 'shoveled into the rear of a truck'. He has his stomach pumped by 'a youngish trim-looking Negro in white jacket and pants' who reappears at various hallucinatory points throughout the novel – and is supposedly discharged from hospital after three days, even though he is now a 'posthumous person'.[9]

In his new, post-traumatic life, Diddy returns to his job working for 'a company that manufactures microscopes'.[10] This is perhaps a nod, as Sontag wrote in her diaries, towards Freud's imagining in *The Interpretation of Dreams* of the part of the mind 'which serves psychic productions' such as dreams as an instrument rather like a 'complicated microscope or camera' – or, instead, a dream-invention or transposition by Diddy of his comatose state in hospital, under medical examination by doctors who peer over and examine him.[11] (Many of the events in the narrative can be read as strangely distorted versions of what is really going on in the hospital.) In a dream in which he falls or is pushed into a hole by his brother Paul, who looks down at him, calling his name, Diddy finds his ex-wife Joan at the bottom, 'but that part of the dream gets dark'.[12] Then he heads upstate by train to a week-long business conference.

In the compartment on the train, Diddy sits near a girl with large 'greenish-black' sunglasses, accompanied by an older woman, her aunt.[13] There is also a priest and a stamp collector – as if Diddy is in an Agatha Christie novel, or Alfred Hitchcock's *North by Northwest*. Is he really on a train, or is the train a metaphysical shuttle hurtling Diddy towards his final, mortal destination? The train speeds on. 'Then, suddenly, the day failed.' The train enters a tunnel. 'The train charged through the darkness, it seemed to go faster, dangerously fast, its motion like a horizontal fall.'[14] The train stops in the tunnel, an inexplicable delay; and Diddy leaves the compartment. He steps off the train. He finds a workman on the track wielding an axe, attempting to clear an obstruction. Diddy kills him, partly out of self-defence, yet otherwise inexplicably, as in Albert Camus' *L'Etranger*. He gets back on the train, his deed undiscovered, and begins talking to the girl as the train starts to move. The girl, Hester, is blind. Diddy confesses his crime to her, but she insists he never left the compartment. They go into the train lavatory together, kiss and have sex, assisted by the rocking of the train.

Once the train has arrived at its destination, the scene is cadaverous, grey and distended, as Diddy waits for his murder to be discovered, but is not apprehended. In the long, monochrome middle section of *Death Kit*, Diddy meets colleagues from the microscope company. He scans the newspapers for news of his crime, but there is nothing but reports of the war far away: 'the drawn-out murder of a small defenceless nation', clearly Vietnam, which puts his own act of murder in perspective and helps Diddy forgive himself, too easily. Eventually there is a report of a man, Incardona, killed by a train in a tunnel. Diddy has a vivid vision of Incardona's autopsy, perhaps really his own, presided over by the 'Negro in white jacket and pants'.[15]

In the waltz-like idyll of the final third of *Death Kit*, Diddy and Hester have a gently surreal love affair. Diddy returns to New York with Hester, and leaves his job, resigning for 'Reasons of health'. In the small apartment they share, they soon begin to quarrel, Hester debilitated by Diddy's demands, as his own 'precious ration of vitality, preserved through such excruciating trials' was 'leaking away'. Diddy becomes bedridden, with Hester his nurse; he takes her with him back into the tunnel where the train stopped, and kills Incardona again. Hester's cries are mixed up with voices from the hospital room – "'Wake up!'", "Hey!", "Try the oxygen!'"[16] Diddy enters a huge gallery or charnel house filled with coffins and corpses, in a virtuoso set-piece at the close of the novel, which finally grants him a peaceful death.

Diddy's killing of Incardona in the tunnel makes *Death Kit* a metaphysical murder story. The killing is also a metaphor for America's role in the Vietnam War, which generated a similarly nightmarish, unreal, confusingly mediated sense of guilt. Diddy, the accidental murderer, is an American everyman, just as everyone in America, Sontag implied, was guilty of what was going on in Vietnam. Despite the Vietnam theme, and Sontag's attempt after *The Benefactor* to move away from solipsism, *Death Kit* reflects the world outside Diddy's skull only distortedly. Yet the theme of moral disquiet in the face of vague awareness of one's implication in atrocity would permeate Sontag's later, historically-focused essays.

Before writing *Death Kit*, Sontag had been thinking of the novel form in cinematic terms, and had made lists of novels with a cinematic structure.[17] *Death Kit* is profoundly filmic (Luis Buñuel expressed an interest in filming it), from its scenes on the train and murder in the tunnel, to its hallucinatory cutting between layers of consciousness and reality, and its awareness of its own fictionality – the name Diddy also references Vladimir's nickname, Didi, in *Waiting for Godot*.[18] The motif of the murder which may or may not have taken place appeared in another film around this time, which also shares a concern with cameras and the framing of reality: Michelangelo Antonioni's *Blow-Up* (1966). *Death Kit* also integrated the contemporary interest in mind-expanding drugs, especially in its skewed sense of being off-centred, out-of-focus. Sontag made several notes in her diaries about acid – noting how LSD caused a visual flattening and loss of depth and also made things visually decompose – relevant to her fictional distortions of time and space in the novel.[19]

While working on *Death Kit*, Sontag was still seeing Jasper Johns, who refreshed her interest in the new theoretical horizons of the 1960s art world. Whereas art was changing monthly, and one had to keep up with new developments – Pop, happenings, Minimalism, Conceptual art – in literature everything remained to be explored, Sontag wrote in her diary.[20] Through Jasper, Sontag spent time not only with Robert Rauschenberg, Merce Cunningham and John Cage, but also with Marcel Duchamp – Cage was getting to know Duchamp, playing chess with him regularly, and Johns and Rauschenberg first met Duchamp in 1959.[21] The anti-psychological bias of Sontag's early essays, the belief in surface and objects, was not only a response to Freud's psychological over-interpretation, but shared these artists' rejection of Abstract Expressionism's cult of the individual. In an interview, Sontag looked back on this period when she spent time with all these figures: 'it was terrifically liberating for me to be with these people and hear their babble.'[22]

In January 1966, Sontag also met the reclusive artist Joseph Cornell, who had developed a fascination with Sontag a few years before, renewed after reading her review of Maurice Nadeau's *The History of Surrealism* in *Book Week*. After sending Sontag a copy of his film script *Monsieur Phot* (1933), Cornell visited her apartment in Greenwich Village. Sontag became the subject of several of Cornell's boxes – little worlds of Surrealist collage that explored themes of artifice, myth, glamour, icons, theatricality, the stars of stage and screen, through radical and often startlingly beautiful juxtapositions. Cornell lived with his mother and his brother Robert in a house on Utopia Parkway in Queens, where he had a workshop in the basement; he fell in love often and created fan packages for the objects of his devotion.

One of the collages he made for Sontag focused on a nineteenth-century diva, Henriette Sontag;[23] another, focusing on Sontag herself, was entitled *The Ellipsian* (1966), and framed a scuffed, torn book-jacket photograph of Sontag from *The Benefactor* in the top-right corner of the box, looking regally out across ovals, ellipses and circles echoing a scrap from a chart of the solar system. The portrait is otherworldly, spare, geometric, graceful. It speaks keenly of Cornell's idealization of Sontag; and around the turn of 1965–6 Cornell sent her and David letters, postcards, valentines, Christmas cards, cryptic messages and ephemera, which Sontag kept.[24] Yet Cornell's passion cooled, or was rebuffed: having made several gifts of his to Sontag, he sent a messenger to take some of them back. Cornell, in his sixties, was not an obvious suitor for Sontag: his one recorded intimate experience with a woman, a shared bath together, took place only after his mother died.[25]

Against Interpretation came out early in 1966, consolidating Sontag's stature as a critic; she was still writing *Death Kit*, which came quickly, but not easily. Being with Jasper, Sontag thought, was good for her, yet she still saw herself as alone since Irene, only really living for David, perhaps drying out a little emotionally, her singleness becoming worryingly normal for her. She planned to go to Europe for the summer – London, Paris, Czechoslovakia,

Joseph Cornell, *The Ellipsian*, 1966, mixed media.

Antibes, Venice. Her European travels were becoming a yearly fixture, although she was not yet as habituated to France as she would become. This year, she took David.

In July, as part of her research for the charnel house ending of *Death Kit*, Susan and David visited the Catacombs of Paris, an underground ossuary in a network of tunnels beneath the city, holding the remains of several million people, their bones ordered and displayed on the walls, open to visitors since the early nineteenth century. In the catacombs, death was aestheticized, Sontag noted in her diaries, offering no single interpretation to the wandering visitor but a medley of beliefs, akin to the grisly yet awe-inspiring 'inventory of the world' Diddy perceives at the close of *Death Kit*.[26] The ending of the novel, inspired also by Sontag's friend Peter Hujar's photographs of the Palermo Catacombs, was now in sight.[27] Hujar had visited the Palermo Catacombs in 1963 with Paul Thek, who was likewise heavily influenced by them. While Sontag was writing *Death Kit*, Thek made a strikingly analogous artwork, *The Tomb*, an installation first exhibited in 1967, the centrepiece of which was a body cast of the artist, dead, painted pink, surrounded by offerings to the afterlife, which, like *Death Kit*, also symbolized the dark side of the 1960s dream.

Sontag flew from Paris to Prague, then went on to Karlovy-Vary, staying for ten days before driving with Elliott Stein back to the Czech capital. One Saturday morning in the Hotel Ambassador in Prague, writing in her diary in the lobby while David slept upstairs, she felt the first glimmers of contentment for some time.[28]

In August, Sontag sat in on a collaboration in London between Peter Brook and Jerzy Grotowski's theatre companies. Sontag was always fascinated by the figure of the guru, and watching these charismatic theatre directors influenced her later depictions of power relations in the films *Duet for Cannibals* and *Brother Carl*, and helped her years later when she herself directed plays. Brook was a 'brain-picker', Sontag wrote, 'very intense, high-pitched'. Grotowski, she thought, was like Caligari or the musician in Thomas Mann's *Mario and the Magician*.[29] Both men were very different to Sontag's more easy-going, 'Beat' friend Joe Chaikin, of the Living Theatre, to whom her next book of essays, *Styles of Radical Will*, would be dedicated. Seeing Brook and Grotowski also prompted Sontag to think again about selfhood and identity. She even thought of completing her abandoned doctorate. Her potential thesis topic now was 'Self-Consciousness, Consciousness of Self, and

Self-Transcendence in Contemporary French Philosophy' – covering writers including Henri Bergson, Jean-Paul Sartre, Georges Bataille, Maurice Blanchot and Gaston Bachelard.[30] The thesis was never written, although its themes would continue to influence her. After London, Sontag flew back to Paris, seeing Godard filming *Deux ou trois choses que je sais d'elle*;[31] she took the train to Antibes, then went on to Venice, staying in the Gritti Palace Hotel. Back in New York, she went over *Death Kit*. The novel was finished in time to be published the following summer, of 1967.

The essays Sontag wrote around this time, collected in *Styles of Radical Will*, are more intense, oblique explorations of their subjects than anything in *Against Interpretation*. There are eight long pieces in *Styles of Radical Will*, as opposed to the more miscellaneous 26 pieces of the earlier book. They are less fractured, less stop-and-start in form. The fusion of high and low culture – there is nothing as flashy as 'Notes on "Camp"' – was no longer Sontag's essayistic signature. *Styles of Radical Will* centres more exclusively on generally 'high', European, avant-garde subjects: 'The Aesthetics of Silence', E. M. Cioran, 'Theatre and Film', Bergman's *Persona*, and Godard, with a flourish at something more outré in a discussion of literary pornography in Bataille, Sade, Pauline Réage's *Story of O* and Jean de Berg's *The Image* (the last two texts both written under pseudonyms).

Sontag was still interested in the interplay between genres and art forms but mostly avoided writing about fiction, while the pieces on Bergman and Godard continued her fascination with cinema. All the pieces showed her continued slant against interpretation, being concerned with form and style rather than excavation of meaning; yet they went further towards analysis, and showed more of a personal, appropriative interest in storytelling, narrative and artistic strategies. The newest note in *Styles of Radical Will* was the inclusion of two political pieces: the strident, slightly shrill 'What's Happening in America' – initially a response to a questionnaire from the editors of *Partisan Review* – and the more searching account of Sontag's 'Trip to Hanoi' in 1968.

In 'The Aesthetics of Silence', Sontag elaborates on the ideas she had developed in her diaries for a novel about an artist devoted to a spiritual project. Once again, the essay owes much to her teaching of religion. 'Every era has to reinvent the project of "spirituality" for itself', Sontag writes. 'In the modern era, one of the most active metaphors for the spiritual project is "art".'[32] Sontag was always attuned to the subliminal shifts in broad cultural values that forced the artist to play new roles in society; her interest in the 'spiritual project' of post-Duchamp art also echoes and extends, more positively, the idea of the saintly, suffering writer outlined in 'The Artist as Exemplary Sufferer' and 'Simone Weil' in *Against Interpretation*.

The essay on silence deals with the turn towards renunciation, nothingness and absence as an artistic strategy in the work of various twentieth-century artists, anti-artists, philosophers, playwrights, musicians and writers, referencing Duchamp's readymades; Cage's $4'33''$ and use of chance operations; suicides such as Kleist's and Lautréamont's; madmen such as Hölderlin and Artaud; and exemplary renunciations of the artistic vocation such as Rimbaud's exile in Abyssinia, Wittgenstein's work as a hospital orderly and Duchamp's 'retirement' from art to play chess. This was a broad definition of silence, to be sure, yet in all of these examples, Sontag suggests, the sense of absence (despite the impossibility of pure silence) plays an important role in art's long-standing function as 'a technique for focusing attention, for teaching skills of attention'.[33]

> Once the artist's task seemed to be simply that of opening up new areas and objects of attention. That task is still acknowledged, but it has become problematic. The very faculty of attention has come into question, and been subjected to more

rigorous standards. As Jasper Johns says: 'Already it's a great deal to see anything *clearly*, for we don't see *anything* clearly'.[34]

The critic's task, too, lies in opening up new areas and objects of attention, as well as fine-tuning the quality of that attention itself. Sontag's criticism does both these things, usually at the same time. In the essay on silence, Sontag continues lines of thought she first explored in 'Against Interpretation', which likewise extolled a sharpening of the senses through refocusing. Yet the minimalism and reduction Sontag encourages serves a self-potentiality which was voracious: 'Ideally, one should be able to pay attention to everything.' Sontag's critical focus was nothing if not ambitious, even over-reaching; and all the pieces in *Styles of Radical Will* show her pushing herself beyond herself, striving. Another shared concern of all the pieces is the problem of language itself, 'the most impure, the most contaminated, the most exhausted of all the materials out of which art is made'. 'We lack words, and we have too many of them', Sontag writes.[35] This was the conundrum recognized and transformed into more words, more writing, through irony, by Beckett, Burroughs, Kafka and Stein – the now-familiar roll-call of Sontag's 1960s canon.

The problematics of writing also inform Sontag's essay on Cioran, 'Thinking Against Oneself', less on the level of the individual utterance than in wider philosophical arguments, and in the structure of essays. The attraction of the aphorism for Cioran, Sontag declares, offering a summation that also reflects the jagged, electric movements of her own aphoristic essay style, lay in its ability to outwit itself: 'For Cioran the aphoristic style is less a principle of reality than a principle of knowing: that it's the destiny of every profound idea to be quickly checkmated by another idea, which it itself has implicitly generated.'[36] In this essay Sontag also inveighs against the spectre of 'historical consciousness'[37] which makes all thinking terminal, ruinous; yet as she grew older she would turn back towards the past more herself, less in thrall to the mute, the object, the uninterpretable, the anti-psychological, the extreme – common tonal and thematic threads throughout *Styles of Radical Will*.

The essays again allowed Sontag to explain the techniques of her fiction, without seeming to be doing so. This is especially the case with the pieces on film. In 'Bergman's *Persona*' and 'Godard', Sontag's interest in both film-makers' strategies describes many of her own ruses in *Death Kit* and *The Benefactor*. '*Persona* is strewn with signs that cancel each other', Sontag writes of Bergman's film, which, like *Death Kit*, confuses illusion and reality, leaving both uncertain. 'Hallucinations or visions will appear on the screen with the same rhythms, the same look of objective reality as something "real".' *Persona* also radically questions representations of character, offering not so much a completed narrative than the 'kit' to make one. As in *Death Kit*, it offers the ingredients of a story alongside the story itself; the narrative can be reconfigured. 'Instead of a full-blown story', Bergman 'presents something that is, in one sense, cruder and, in another, more abstract: a body of material, a subject'.[38]

Sontag pursues a similar interest in abstraction in 'Godard', alongside the film-maker's use of clashing styles, his absorption of swathes of culture. She is intrigued by the 'suppression of certain explicative connections' in his work: 'while the sequence of events in a Godard film suggests a fully articulated story, it doesn't add up to one; the audience is presented with a narrative line that is partly erased or effaced.'[39] Bergman and Godard use different kinds of abstraction, Sontag writes: *Persona* has a 'systematically "indeterminate" plot', while Godard's films use '"intermittent" plots', as parts appear to have been rubbed out.[40] Both film-makers were representative of a new kind of narrative – other filmic examples Sontag mentions are Resnais' *Last Year at Marienbad* and Antonioni's *L'Avventura* – which courted enigma, and calculatedly frustrated 'the desire to know'.[41] One might term such narratives 'abstract realism', though they are usually linked with the New Wave in film and the *nouveau roman* in literature.

Death Kit was published in August 1967, and Susan went to Martinique the same month. The novel had a rough ride in the press; many of the reviewers were not only uncomprehending, but slightly mocking. Sontag's stature as a critic, it seemed, made people expect more from her novels, which suffered in comparison to her essays. The critical response to Sontag's work was now hardening and, to her chagrin, was set for the rest of her life: she was seen as a better critic than novelist, perhaps even a writer whose novels were insufficient precisely because her critical gift was so strong. She herself resented this, always seeing herself as a novelist first, an essayist second, even though it would take two and a half decades after *Death Kit* for her to publish another novel.

With hindsight, *The Benefactor* and *Death Kit* can be seen to have been crucially misunderstood: they are both experiments in 'abstract realism' that, like Duchamp's work in art, exist very powerfully as endlessly reconstructable puzzles. Yet the indeterminacy of both novels, with so much seeming real and yet not quite real, lacks a compelling sense of causality. The sense of endless possibility and potentiality which is so inspiring in Sontag's essays makes her early novels seem reluctant to fully commit themselves. It took Sontag years to come to terms with this.

In Martinique, Sontag wrote a series of reflections on her past in her diaries, still musing over the break with Irene, and her relationship with Mildred when she was growing up. She berated her mother's neediness during her youth, and how their relationship was more sisterly than parental. Sontag was also, in the extended self-analysis of the Martinique diaries, extremely critical of herself, ushering in a new theme in her work: that of the cannibal, or vampire. This was reminiscent of Henry James's

The Sacred Fount, Sontag knew – James had long been the master of the so-called 'vampire theme' – and it was already present in Sontag's essay on *Persona*.

Did Susan use people in her relationships, her love affairs? Did she drain them? Did she pull all the substance out of people, and then move on? 'I feel I'm a vampire, a cannibal', she wrote; she felt she had been 'scavenging' in all her relations – with Merrill, with Philip, with Harriet, with Irene. 'Gathering my treasure, I learn what they know . . . then I take off.'[42] All her relationships did feed into her work: was this the source of its vitality? Susan's writing, like all writing, derived strength from other books; but it also had roots in other people's talk and interests – which kept it fresh. What exactly, then, did Susan take? From Philip, the academic rigour, the stern tone, the command of philosophy, the interest in Freud and interpretation; from Harriet, the understanding of gay life in San Francisco and Paris, which fed into 'Notes on "Camp"'; from Irene, the new ease in her sexuality and interest in theatre; from Jasper, the understanding of the art world, of silence, objects, things simply being as they are. The pattern would continue in later relationships. Sontag led several different creative lives, as critic, as novelist, as playwright, as film-maker. Each of these lives can be traced back to a specific person.

In April 1968, Sontag was unexpectedly invited to go on a two-week visit to North Vietnam, with the journalist Andrew Kopkind and the anti-war activist Robert Greenblatt. She accepted the invitation, as she wrote in 'Trip to Hanoi', 'with the pretty firm idea that I wouldn't write about the trip on my return'.[43] The journey to Vietnam proved a crucial turning point for Sontag, opening up her political consciousness. She had attended a 'Read-in for Peace in Vietnam' in February 1966, with other contemporary writers including Robert Lowell, Norman Mailer and Bernard Malamud; in 1967 she had been arrested at a 'Stop the Draft Week Protest' in New York, alongside Allen Ginsberg, Grace Paley and others. But it was the Vietnam trip that made Sontag see the gaps in her political, cultural and historical awareness.

It also opened her up as a writer. In 'Trip to Hanoi' Sontag wrote for the first time, apart from in her private diaries, in the first person; this, she later said, was 'the first time I ever wrote about myself *at all*'. 'It changed me. I realized I could have a certain freedom as a writer.'[44] Writing about the trip was also an experiment in a new form – the book-length essay – that resurfaced in Sontag's later work, as she wrote similar stand-alone extended essays such as *Illness as Metaphor* (1978) and *Regarding the Pain of Others* (2003). In the preface to the Vietnamese translation of 'Trip to Hanoi', Sontag emphasized how it inaugurated a turn in her thought: 'Everything that I have written now seems to group itself as before or after "Trip to Hanoi".'[45]

The journey to Vietnam was Sontag's first trip East, and her first trip to a war zone of this scale. Travel, for Susan, often meant the European summers she enjoyed throughout her life: feasts of aesthetic pleasure, disorientation, art, treasures; the delirium of wandering and sightseeing celebrated in her short story 'Unguided Tour': 'tile roofs, timbered balconies, fish in the bay, the copper clock, shawls drying on the rocks, the delicate odor of olives, sunsets behind the bridge, ochre stone'.[46] In Vietnam, however, she was travelling to a war she had experienced vicariously through news reports for several years, and had even themed part of *Death Kit* around. The place was so alive in her imagination that actually being there was initially a disappointment. But the trip did force 'an active confrontation with the limits of my own thinking'; and in her attempts to understand the Vietnamese mentality and way of life, Sontag 'came back from Hanoi considerably chastened'.[47]

'Trip to Hanoi' bristles with contradictions and gauche assertions of Sontag's superiority as an American – in her relative, even if comparatively decadent, complexity – to the Vietnamese. But in framing so prominently her own insecurity, her inability to communicate or to contextualize, and by qualifying and modulating nearly all her initial perceptions, Sontag succeeded in turning the piece into an unsettling account of cultural dislocation and failed understanding. 'When I was honest with myself,' she wrote – and the piece is refreshingly honest, unafraid to not be politically correct – 'I had to admit that the place was simply too foreign, that I really understood nothing at all, except at a "distance".'[48]

Even the journey itself was an ordeal, taking ten days because of failed connections in transit, as the odd trio of Sontag, Kopkind and Greenblatt went from New York via Paris and Phnom Penh to Vientiane and Hanoi. (The return trip took just less than a week.) In 'Trip to Hanoi' Sontag quotes from her journal entries to convey the futility and despair in communication she felt in her first days there, as well as her wonder, and the difficult sense she had of the whole trip being stage-managed by the Vietnamese, a 'piece of political theatre'. The interest in the difficulties of language, so prevalent throughout *Styles of Radical Will*, became real during Sontag's stay in Hanoi, not only through her failure to really talk through a translator but in the repetitions of political doublespeak and sloganeering which she heard. She felt uncomfortable in her role as a spectator. She admired and was confused by the strong sense of '*felt* history' in Vietnam. She felt the polluted, hungry depths of her own Americanness, 'the barrier between them and me'. She felt she was in 'a glass box'.[49]

Sontag wandered around the city, sometimes alone, enjoying the attention she stirred up in the Vietnamese. Visits were planned by her guides every morning and afternoon. She chafed at being herded around in this way, being driven everywhere, and at the huge meals she was served at her hotel, the Thong Nat, while most of the Vietnamese around her had so little to eat. But as 'Trip to Hanoi' goes on, Sontag's 'psychic cramp' dissipates, and she begins to reflect, sceptical of her own tentative assumptions, on the ethical and moral attributes of the Vietnamese compared to the Americans, their extraordinary capacities for dealing with suffering, their physical austerity and community-mindedness, the lack of a split between public and private space in their society.[50] She also notes the humbling moral grace in how the Vietnamese granted crashed American bomber pilots proper burials, and the resourcefulness of a people who had constructed more than 21,000,000 bomb shelters since 1965, and were able to find a use for everything.

> Each plane that's shot down is methodically taken apart. The tires are cut up to make the rubber sandals that most people wear. Any component of the engine that's still intact is modified to be reused as part of a truck motor. The body of the plane is dismantled, and the metal is melted down to be made into tools, small machine parts, surgical instruments, wire, spokes for bicycle wheels, combs, ashtrays, and of course the famous numbered rings given as presents to visitors. Every last nut, bolt, and screw from the plane is used. The same holds for anything else the Americans drop. In several hamlets we visited, the bell hanging from a tree which summoned people to meetings or sounded the air-raid alert was the casing of an unexploded bomb.[51]

There was plenty about Vietnam and the Vietnamese which Sontag failed to grasp during her two-week trip, and she was self-consciously aware that the muted idealization of the country she offered in the second half of 'Trip to Hanoi' was probably a distorted response. Radical in her artistic agendas at this period in her life – *Styles of Radical Will* is her most deliberately extreme collection of essays – Sontag was determined to be equally radical in her engagement with politics. As she wrote up her trip after her return from Vietnam, over June and July 1968, other events took place for which she must have felt sympathies: May 1968 in France, and the Prague Spring. 'An event that makes new feelings conscious is always the most important experience a person can have', Sontag wrote. 'These days, it's a pressing moral imperative as well.'[52]

Her interior journey in Hanoi was misguided mostly by her own indignation and deeply inherited attitudes – a visit to American prisoners of war in Hanoi, for instance, recorded in her diaries and hinting at the torture they endured, was not included in 'Trip to Hanoi', since it contradicted Sontag's anger over the American bombings, about which she did not want to be appeased, whatever she saw. The trip was too short, and the idealization of the Vietnamese, though well meaning, was patronizing. But Sontag made the experience transformative, starting her own revolution of self: 'So I discover what happened to me in North Vietnam did not end with my return to America, but is still going on.'[53] Once again, travel had changed her; for the first time the desire she had been expressing for so long, to engage with the world, had become a reality.

5

In Plato's Cave, 1968–1975

She was not in America for long; almost as soon as she had returned to New York, Sontag was off again on her travels, heading to Europe for the summer of 1968. With David now a teenager, she was becoming more rootless than ever before, or rather, she was putting down new roots that shifted her centre of identity, in particular as she became more resident in Paris, as opposed to the yearly visitor she had been for so long. Her Parisian world became distinctively French, rather than American, as it had been initially. Yet while she was becoming more known in the city's artistic and literary circles, she was often elsewhere in Europe. That summer she also went to Italy, where she hoped to find a producer for a new project – another radical departure – a film.

Just as Sontag's geographical centre was shifting, so too was her chosen creative medium: she was devoted to film-making for the next few years. While visiting Rome in July, she received an invitation to visit Stockholm from Göran Lindgren of Sandrew Film & Teater. Sandrew offered to produce Sontag's first film, and Sontag stayed in Sweden for the next five months, writing and directing *Duet for Cannibals*.

The invitation, and Sontag's immediate acceptance of it, did not come out of nowhere. There were important European precedents – most obviously Marguerite Duras, Pier Paolo Pasolini and Alain Robbe-Grillet – for writers turning film directors. In 'Against Interpretation' Sontag had written that 'cinema is the most alive, the most exciting, the most important of all art forms right now.'[1] As a critic, she had been deeply interested in the European tradition outlined in the 1960s in her essays on film, on Bergman, Bresson, Godard and Resnais. This was the lineage she drew from in her own films. But she was also steeped in American underground film-making, and might as easily have become a homegrown avant-garde film-maker like Jack Smith (whose *Flaming Creatures* Sontag discussed in *Against Interpretation*), Kenneth Anger, Stan Brakhage, Maya Deren or Jonas Mekas, all of whose work she knew. That Sontag went to Sweden instead was due to force of circumstance, as the offer of production came from Lindgren; however, Sweden also offered another artistic liberation from depicting contemporary American life, that source of so much discomfort for Sontag and a subject she found hard to depict fictionally. The cultural disjunction also suited her idea, noted in July 1968 in Paris, for making a film about language.[2]

Sweden was hardly as far from Sontag's American experience as Vietnam; yet in the two films she made there with mostly Swedish actors, one (*Duet for Cannibals*) filmed in Swedish with English subtitles, the other (*Brother Carl*) in English, the themes of language and the failure to communicate, silence, muteness and renunciation all figure largely. Both films continue Sontag's exploration of abstract realism in her fiction. But they are more emotionally charged than *The Benefactor* and *Death Kit*, being centred on tales of couples, anatomizing the dynamics of contemporary sexual relationships in a far more direct way.

The new medium brought out different abilities and interests. While both films were enigmatic and unconventional, they offer a glimpse of a type of novelist Sontag never became: a writer committed to creating emotional situations purely out of relations between characters, in which abstraction serves to heighten emotion by removing everything else. In film, Sontag found new narrative inclinations, aligned more closely with the private material in her diaries about her love affairs. Her films also continue, in an elliptical way, the radical dissatisfactions in her 'Notes on Marriage'.

Sontag wrote the script for *Duet for Cannibals* in Stockholm in August 1968, and finished a second version in September, while completing the casting and choosing the locations. She filmed the entire movie over six weeks in October and November, using fairly minimal equipment: one Arriflex camera and a Nagra for recording dialogue. Of the seven-strong cast, all were Scandinavian apart from the Italian Adriana Astri. Given Sontag's interest in the chance aesthetic of John Cage, and the polyglot, improvisatory feel of Godard's films, her first experience of film-making, she thought, would be open to happy accidents during the course of shooting, and interventions from members of the cast and crew. In the event, the actors stuck closely to the script, with little improvisation. Perhaps because of this, *Duet for Cannibals* has a taut, 'written' quality; a classical – or minimalist – sense of design. There is a neatness to the plotting which is strangely ordered, but the events the film depicts are extremely discomfiting, producing an effect of surrealistic anxiety (and black humour): 'the anxiety produced when familiar things aren't in their place or playing their accustomed role', as Sontag put it in 'The Aesthetics of Silence', writing of the puzzling bareness of Beckett and Kafka.[3]

Duet for Cannibals is set in Stockholm in an 'abstract present' day.[4] The action follows two couples – two 'ex-students' in their twenties, Tomas and Ingrid, and Arthur Bauer, in his middle or late forties, a political radical and intellectual (he treasures a cigarette lighter given to him by Brecht) in exile with his younger wife Francesca. Tomas goes to work for Bauer in his villa outside Stockholm: like much else in the script, the precise nature of the work is vague, but it involves assisting Bauer in cataloguing his papers, as if in order to help him write his memoirs. 'I don't know what ever possessed me to undertake this project', Bauer tells Tomas. 'Reviewing one's whole life is a formidable task. And there are so many secrets I can't reveal.'[5] Bauer asks Tomas to stay at the house while they work on the cataloguing and, as part of the job, he also asks Tomas to look after Francesca, who on first meeting Tomas throws a book through a closed window, and then over several later scenes begins to seduce him.

Ingrid and Tomas's relationship, from the beginning of *Duet for Cannibals*, is failing, becoming strained: the couple are unable to talk to each other properly. They both seem half-formed, innocent, uneasy. Ingrid is also troubled by Tomas's work at the Bauer house, where events become increasingly unsettling. Francesca wakes Tomas on his bed in the library one night and shows him a tape recorder locked in a cupboard. When Tomas later plays the tape, he hears Bauer talking about his imminent death. 'I can feel the disease getting worse. The doctors promised me at least two years . . .

Francesca showing Tomas the tape recorder in *Duet for Cannibals* (1969).

but I suspect they were wrong.'[6] Another night, Bauer wakes Tomas (there is a suspicion these nightly wakings are in fact dreams); Francesca has locked herself in the car, where the Bauers eventually make love in front of Tomas.

The games between the Bauers and Tomas become more sinister: Francesca gives Tomas a gun and asks him to kill her husband, and Tomas hears Bauer on the tape: 'I've decided to do away with Francesca . . . It pains me, but – '.[7] After Tomas and Francesca sleep together, with Bauer trapped in the closet, Bauer sets out to seduce Ingrid. In a surrealistic parody of a bourgeois dinner party, the two couples dine together, and Ingrid is offered the role of 'amateur servant' after Bauer suddenly fires the housekeeper, Mrs Grundberg, suspecting that the food is poisoned.[8] Ingrid ends up in bed with both the Bauers, almost as part of her 'duties'. Towards the end, Bauer pretends to Tomas that he has killed Francesca, and then kills himself. But Tomas sees them both standing at the window looking down when he leaves, after he and Ingrid have joyfully made a bonfire of Bauer's papers in the garden.

In Sontag's first conception of the film, Bauer was not a political exile but a psychiatrist, and Tomas was his assistant. This, Sontag later realized in her diaries, was a transmutation of her earlier, abandoned 'Thomas Faulk' project, in which Thomas was a patient in a private clinic, not a young doctor – but the name Thomas remained.[9] In *Duet for Cannibals* it is never clear whether Tomas is really assisting the Bauers or merely being played with by them as he enters their web, like the ball of string in the curious scene where the Bauers sit opposite each other, Francesca winding yarn into a ball while Bauer holds the yarn for her to wind.

Duet for Cannibals, more than Sontag's earlier novels, takes place in a real environment, yet it still inhabits what Sontag called 'an imaginary psychological universe; partly realistic in the sense of everyday psychology and partly a kind of fantastic psychology which I also believe is true – yet not true on the level of plausibilities

The Bauers at the window in *Duet for Cannibals* (1969).

of daily life'.[10] The film is a pure play of forces, of strength and
weakness, as the Bauers devour Tomas and Ingrid psychologically
and sexually, weaker selves being rolled up into stronger ones.
The film is a modern, deliberately twisted recapitulation of James's
'vampire' theme; it dramatizes Sontag's anxieties about her own
voracity, and her evolving ethical sense of wisdom as being tainted,
of purity being innocent, and the impossibility of wanting – as she
did – to be both wise and pure.[11] She always felt she 'ate' books as if

they were food, and worried about this tendency; she likewise associated eating with sexuality. The disquiet around eating in *Duet for Cannibals* also arose from Sontag's awareness of her American appetite (cultural and physical) throughout 'Trip to Hanoi', the 'gluttonous habits of my consciousness'.[12] Sontag extracts queasy black humour from this as Bauer greedily, hilariously gobbles his food at dinner, to Tomas's amazement and revulsion, then leaves the table to vomit off-screen. 'It's nothing. Believe me. Go on eating,' Francesca assures Tomas, before Bauer returns to his seat and serves himself another large portion.[13]

Bauer also swallows Tomas up intellectually. Tomas, in his role cataloguing Bauer's papers, is like a biographer, swamped by his subject. *Duet for Cannibals* dramatizes the power relations in biography, as young Tomas enters the house and becomes privy to secrets and to his subject's domestic life, while his own life is put to one side. In what could be an in-joke from Sontag to future biographers, Tomas, making stacks of Bauer's notebooks in his study, finds gaps in the notebooks from 1953, just as Sontag's notebooks likewise fall silent at this time after her marriage to Philip Rieff. Indeed there are, perhaps subconscious, similarities between Bauer and Rieff. Meeting Philip, Sontag swooned in her diaries at the chance 'to *do* some research work' for the older Rieff, in an initially slightly servile literary role which mirrors Tomas's relation to the older Dr Bauer.[14] Tomas is likewise told by Bauer, 'I'm giving you a chance to *do* something.'[15] For many years, Susan had indeed been swallowed up by Philip; when she re-emerged she was, like Tomas, finally stronger for her experiences, while Philip suffered.

Once the filming of *Duet for Cannibals* was finished, Sontag was travelling again, giving a talk in December 1968 at the National University of Mexico in Mexico City, where students and lecturers were inflamed by the massacre of 2 October, during which protesters had been jailed, beaten and shot, following on from the army occupation of the universities in September. Under intense questioning from the thousand-strong audience in Mexico, Sontag started to cry: as in Vietnam, confronted with the complexity of international political situations, she was slightly floundering.[16]

In January 1969 she went to Cuba for two weeks, resulting in a piece for *Ramparts*, 'Some Thoughts on the Right Way (for Us) to Love the Cuban Revolution'. Largely positive about the revolution at this time, marvelling at the energy that had persisted there since her visit with Irene a decade before, Sontag drew contrasts between the Cuban situation and the radical Left in America. Sontag changed her stance on Cuba two years later, when she realized the extent to which Castro had persecuted writers and political opponents; her convictions shifted even further later on. In the *Ramparts* essay, Sontag declared: 'no Cuban writer has been or is in jail, or is failing to get his work published.'[17] She soon realized that this was not true.

Sontag edited *Duet for Cannibals* during February, and showed the first print of the finished film to Lindgren, alone, one Saturday morning in Stockholm in March. Lindgren liked the film, he told her, on emerging from the screening room; she was 'welcome' in Sweden next year to make another film. In May *Duet for Cannibals* premiered at Cannes, and Sontag showed it in September at the New York Film Festival, appearing on television alongside the French director Agnès Varda in an interview with *Newsweek*'s Jack Kroll. Sontag spent most of the summer of 1969, however, in Italy. She was working out the plot of her next film in her head all that summer; she was also involved in a new romance, with the Italian aristocrat Carlotta del Pezzo, which swept her completely away.

Sontag felt intense 'passion, hope, longing' in her new liaison with Carlotta that July and August. The affair was a seismic emotional event for Susan after the lingering loneliness since Irene which she tried, with great effort, to displace. From the start, she invested more in Carlotta than was wise. In Sontag's diaries,

Carlotta emerges as a dissociated, ambivalent presence, reluctant to fully commit herself personally and embroiled in a previous romance with another lover, Beatrice. At eighteen, Carlotta told Susan, she had started taking heroin, and she felt that her anxiety was such that without heroin, she would have committed suicide. She had since overcome her addiction – a 'heroic' act, thought Susan, for which Carlotta never allowed herself to take full credit.[18]

Carlotta's moods were overwhelming, although she was a very gentle person. As Sigrid Nunez observed a few years later, Carlotta was 'easy-going' but 'prone to depressions that left her nearly catatonic'.[19] Meeting Beatrice in Naples that summer, Sontag was warned by Carlotta's former lover that Carlotta was extremely fragile. Sontag felt herself to be the polar opposite of Carlotta. Where Sontag was will-driven, decisive, independent, addicted to plans, the future and her work, Carlotta was fatalistic, unable to master her feelings, less project-focused (although she worked for the fashion designer Ken Scott), preferring to go with the flow. 'Don't you see that you are the author of your life?'[20] Susan told Carlotta one day in Milan. Carlotta disagreed. The two temperaments were incompatible; yet for a time they were happy.

The relationship was not helped by distance. After Italy, Sontag returned to New York in September, and began work on the script of *Brother Carl* with her assistant and friend Florence Malraux, the daughter of André Malraux and wife of Alain Resnais. By this time, Sontag's place in New York was no longer in Greenwich Village but the two-bedroom penthouse on the corner of 106th Street and Riverside Drive, '340', which remained her American base for most of the 1970s. The previous tenant had been Jasper Johns; Sontag took over the lease when he left.[21] The large windows of the apartment looked out over the Hudson, with wonderful views of the sunset. The decor was generally sparse and ascetic, although the corridors were lined with books, and there were film stills and photographs of Sontag's literary heroes on the walls. In Sontag's bedroom, where she worked, the walls were kept deliberately bare, the space kept free of books, in order not to distract her from the writing to be done at the table with her IBM Selectric.[22] Away from Carlotta, writing *Brother Carl* with Florence, Sontag entered a new phase in their relationship: of 'intensified longing, obsession, suffering' over Carlotta, as she waited patiently to be reunited with her.[23]

A terrible shock came during the writing, in November 1969. Sontag's friend Susan Taubes – whom Sontag had always regarded as her double, ever since they first met and while they worked together teaching at Columbia – killed herself. One evening, Susan Taubes had left her home near the university, where she still taught, and taken the train to Long Island, then a taxi to the beach. Wearing black slacks and a ski jacket, according to newspaper reports, she walked out into the water of the Atlantic Ocean and drowned.[24] She was 41, and she had just published her first novel, *Divorcing*, which drew on her split from her husband Jacob Taubes – Jacob, who had seen Sontag off so touchingly when she left by boat for England in 1957.

Sontag helped to identify the body of her friend.[25] In her short story 'Debriefing', written a few years later, Sontag fictionalized Susan Taubes as the character Julia, anxious, thin, neurotic, unable to eat or go out, taunted by impossible thoughts.

That late Wednesday afternoon, I told Julia how stupid it would be if she committed suicide. She agreed. I thought I was convincing. Two days later she left her apartment again and killed herself.

The story is an elegy to the friend she made, at nineteen years old, on the steps of the Widener Library at Harvard: 'so thin; so prettily affected; so electric; so absent . . . so tired already; so exasperating; so moving'.[26] Susan was profoundly distressed by the other Susan's death. Yet it made her more determined to keep on living. In her diaries, she thought about writing a philosophical dialogue on suicide, entitled 'Reasons for Being'.[27] This was never written, but the suicide made its way into the script of *Brother Carl*.

Brother Carl had a slower gestation than *Duet for Cannibals*, and was also more pensive in mood. The anarchic note of comedy in the first film was absent in *Brother Carl*, which is earnestly spiritual, brooding and sombre, while also more concerned with purity and brightness. Sontag envisaged *Brother Carl* as 'a winter's tale',[28] which, she argued with a sceptical Lindgren, simply *had* to be shot in black-and-white rather than colour: indeed, she saw the whole film as a movement from darkness to light. The story hinges on a dark deed in the past, never told, redeemed by an opposing gift at the close of the film, a miracle. 'The only interesting action in life is a miracle or the failure to perform a miracle', Sontag wrote in the preface to the script.[29] In her diaries while writing the film, Sontag found herself wrestling with the complexity of the characters and themes, which circled around suffering and sanctity, love and moral corruption.[30] *Brother Carl* was initially to build towards two miracles, but only one takes place.

Like *Duet for Cannibals*, it is another tale of dysfunctional couples. The plotting is equally neat and ordered, and the cast was very small: six actors. Most of the action was again shot on location, in this case an island (one of several echoes of Shakespeare's *The Tempest*). Once again the film follows a couple whose relationship is failing – Karen and Peter Sandler – and their difficult intertwinement with another couple, Martin and Lena. Karen and Peter's relationship is marked by 'unconsummated estrangement' and their inability to really talk to each other; this strain is exacerbated and reflected by their six-year-old daughter Anna, who seems autistic, and is mute.[31] Martin and Lena have likewise reached a state of impasse, having been divorced for five years. They share professional interests, as both are theatre directors (Martin of opera); in place of children, the rift in their relationship is embodied in Carl, who was a celebrated dancer in Martin's company, and now appears disturbed, mute like Anna, mentally scarred by the untold thing Martin did to him. Laurent Terzieff, who plays Carl in the film, saw a parallel of Carl and Martin in Nijinsky and Diaghilev. Sontag tells us, in fact, that she had someone else vaguely in mind when depicting Martin (probably Peter Brook or Jerzy Grotowski).

At the outset of *Brother Carl*, Karen and Lena travel together to the island where Martin has a summer house, and where Carl is also staying. As in *Duet for Cannibals*, the characters exchange psychic and sexual energies, although Sontag wanted their relations to be less marked by 'cannibalism' than by a sense of giving and receiving. But they do devour each other. Martin tries repeatedly to seduce Karen, who interests him for her half-formed quality; Lena is trying, without success, to get through to Martin. 'Do you know why I'm here?' Lena asks him. 'Yes.' 'And your answer?' 'No.'[32] Lena sleeps with Carl, in the cave-like cabin where he stays, partly to try and reach Martin, who remains unmoved, unfeeling. Faced by the impassive wall of Martin's indifference, Lena walks into the sea at sunrise on a deserted beach of the island, until the water closes over her head. Carl finds Lena's body. The first, failed, miracle in the film was to be the resurrection of Lena. Instead, Carl takes the mute child Anna down to the edge of the sea, and in a mighty effort which kills him, tries to give her the gift of speech.

Brother Carl ventures further into the terrain of the 'imaginary psychological universe', partly realistic and partly abstract, which Sontag charted in *Duet for Cannibals*, with more grace, solemnity and silence – and with a tragic, rather than darkly comic, approach to emotional and psychological damage. In her essay 'Approaching Artaud' (1973), Sontag would write of Artaud's theatre as being 'a place where the obscure facets of "the spirit" are revealed in "a real, material projection"'.[33] In *Brother Carl*, Sontag wanted to achieve a similar transformation of emotional, sexual and spiritual forces into film. Both Carl and Anna, the two afflicted mute presences, are, more than 'real' characters, emblems of pain and the miscommunications between the couples: almost, walking emotions. In the interchanges between Karen, Martin, Lena and Peter there is again a power play, a sense of vampirism, of stronger and weaker forces in opposition, mirroring the give and take in all relationships.

Hiding places feature largely in *Brother Carl*. As Susan did as a child, Carl digs a hole. He also hides in the recess of an abandoned fort at Rindö, with Anna, as well as in his cabin. Lena perhaps finds the ultimate hiding place, as she walks out to sea. In the script, Karen tells Martin of a dream in which Lena came back to life, and how when she woke up, she thought it had really happened. In her diaries, Sontag wrote that she herself had this dream, about Susan Taubes.[34] 'Some nights, I dream of dragging Julia back by her long hair', Sontag also wrote in 'Debriefing'. 'I look down . . . and seize her by the hair and pull her out.'[35] The actual scene of Lena's death was in the script for *Brother Carl* but never shot; the sequence about Karen's dream was shot but dropped. In the failed resurrection of Lena, the theme of false death in Sontag's work was treated less ambiguously. Death here was finally real, as Susan Taubes's death was real.

After finishing the first draft of the script of *Brother Carl*, Sontag visited Stockholm for two weeks in January 1970, in the depths of the Scandinavian winter, to begin casting and choosing locations. Then she went to Paris for one week, where she spent time with Carlotta, whom she evidently hoped would come to New York with her. Carlotta wavered and backed out of going to America with Susan at the last minute. As Susan reworked *Brother Carl* in New York in the spring of 1970 – not only was the film dedicated to Carlotta but the title, always important for Sontag, almost abbreviated her name – she felt chronically unsettled by Carlotta's loss of heart. In fact, she felt abandoned, as if the initial

Carl pulling Lena out of the water in *Brother Carl* (1971).

innocence of her relationship with Carlotta was now over. The game had changed; the hope of the previous phase of their love was now let down. Slightly panicking, searching for advice, Susan talked with Stephen Koch, Joe Chaikin, Florence Malraux and other friends, about the situation with her Italian lover. She also poured her heart out in her diaries, which always sought to transform pain into progress.

Back in Europe for the summer, Susan saw Carlotta again in Italy; yet the more desperate Susan felt for reassurance, the more Carlotta prevaricated. The strength Carlotta first saw in Susan was part of what attracted her, and Susan was unable to show that strength now. She returned to Stockholm to begin the eight weeks of filming *Brother Carl* throughout August and September. When filming was over she returned to Italy, where relations with Carlotta finally broke down utterly in the first week of October. 'It's over', Susan wrote, devastated, in her diary. The pain was

Sontag in 1971.

overwhelming, shadowed by the fear of loneliness again. But as she turned, as ever, to her journals for self-support, she already knew some of the moves she would make to keep going. Eventually, Susan's strength in picking herself up from the wreckage of her love life would become almost automatic, not always usefully so. But her recoil from the savage disappointment of Carlotta took some time to overcome. She felt she had put herself wholly on the line, tried as hard as she could, and was defeated. Once again, she was alone, and more starkly: 'Perhaps I always will be.'[36]

In the preface to *Brother Carl*, edited and dubbed in the last few months of 1970, Sontag wrote that she had recently been trying in her own life 'to perform a kind of miracle . . . When I started to write the script, I was in the throes of that effort. The week after the end of shooting, in Rome, I learned that I had failed.'[37] The miracle was not – as it might have been – the resurrection of Susan Taubes, but the attempt to win over Carlotta. At the same time, the film marked the end of Sontag's association with Sandrew. She showed the finished print to Lindgren, again alone, in January 1971. The invitation to return to make another film was not repeated.

Over the next two years, Sontag edged towards professional and personal crisis. She found herself slightly adrift as she approached her forties. Without meaning to, she had ceased to be a writer of critical essays and fiction since 1968, becoming more a film-maker and political activist. The new directions in her work threatened her central self-definition as a writer. *Death Kit* had been poorly received; the political pieces sometimes made her feel fraudulent; and the reception of *Brother Carl*, Susan felt, was 'disastrous'.[38] The Swedish films had not made her any money; indeed, she went into debt to support herself while making them.[39] Also without really meaning to, she seemed to have become an expatriate, spending more time in Europe than in New York. Like many American writers before her, Henry James and Gertrude Stein among them, Sontag found her muse in France and Europe rather than America, but her solution was not, like theirs, complete expatriation but an endless series of ever-longer trips and returns. This double life, while stimulating, was at times confusing for her, and her placelessness, neither belonging fully to America nor Europe any more but trying to bridge both opposing worlds, was exacerbated by the collapse of her affair with Carlotta.

Hearing of the death of the writer Paul Goodman, whom Sontag knew slightly, prompted her to write a piece about him in September 1972, which later formed the opening to her collection *Under the Sign of Saturn*. The piece begins with a portrait of Sontag herself, in her Paris cave of the early 1970s, lost and trying to begin anew:

> I am writing this in a tiny room in Paris, sitting on a wicker chair at a typing table in front of a window which looks onto a garden; at my back is a cot and a night table; on the floor and under the table are manuscripts, notebooks, and two or three paperback books. That I have been living and working for more than a year in such small bare quarters, though not at the beginning planned or thought out, undoubtedly answers to some need to strip down, to close off for a while, to make a new start with as little as possible to fall back on.[40]

The room was Sontag's pied-à-terre in Paris for several years during the 1970s. It was off the rue de la Faisanderie, a smart address in the sixteenth arrondissement, a little flat above the garage of the house of Nicole Stéphane, who became Susan's first French lover in the wake of the break-up with Carlotta. That Nicole was also a film producer was no accident; as with so many of Susan's affairs (from Philip on), work and love merged. Nicole had produced Marguerite Duras' *Détruire, dit-elle*, screening it at Cannes in 1969, where, possibly, she met Sontag; she was also at Cannes in 1971.[41] She was ten years older than Susan, and she had an extraordinary past.

Nicole Stéphane and Edouard Dermithe in the poster for Jean-Pierre Melville's adaptation of Jean Cocteau's *Les Enfants terribles* (1950).

During the Second World War she fled Paris, in 1942 – she was Jewish, and a descendant of the Rothschild banking family – moving via Spain and Lisbon to London, where she joined the French Resistance. Discovered by Jean-Pierre Melville in drama school after the war, she acted in *Le Silence de la mer* (1949) and *Les Enfants terribles* (1950) in her twenties. Partly because of a car accident in the early 1960s, Nicole stopped her acting career early, becoming a producer. Her taste in films was unashamedly literary: she was involved for several decades in trying to produce a film version of Proust's *A la recherche du temps perdu*. Nicole could be quite maternal in her affections towards the younger Susan; with the relationship also came a greater immersion into French life for Susan, all the more so as Nicole's English was weak.

With Nicole's backing, Sontag developed an adaptation of Simone de Beauvoir's first novel, *L'Invitée*, another tangled tale of couples, one of whose characters reminded Susan of Carlotta.[42] The script of the film was completed, running to nearly 200 pages, and Sontag knew it would be on a larger scale than that of her two tight Swedish films, involving reconstruction of the 1930s setting.[43] But, after all the preparation, *L'Invitée* was never made.

Around this time, however, Sontag did publish two idiosyncratic essays on women, 'The Third World of Women' and 'The Double Standard of Aging', while beginning tentatively, slowly, to start out once more as a fiction writer, working mainly on short stories. After the short reflection on Paul Goodman, she also resumed her role as a critical and cultural essayist with her long piece 'Approaching Artaud' in the *New Yorker*. This essay returned to Sontag's interests in the theatre and in literary modernism, as well as long-standing themes of extremity of consciousness, madness, suffering and Surrealism.

'In Artaud,' Sontag writes, 'the artist as seer crystallizes, for the first time, into the figure of the artist as pure victim of his consciousness.'[44] Artaud's thought, Sontag declares, draws up new maps and frontiers for consciousness that, in their extremity, remain unassimilable – just as his ideas for theatre were largely impossible to stage. The blazing ferocity of Artaud's ideas acted as a purgative on Sontag, and the essay, brilliant in its intensity, was in some ways one long exorcism of the state of near-crisis Sontag felt she had reached.

In her diaries around the same time, she wrote of wanting to start afresh by writing short stories, trying on new styles and voices as well as facing up squarely to her artistic problems.[45] Around ten years before, in 1964, she had noted that 'writing is a little door' – not everything she wanted would squeeze through it. This, as with all limitations for Sontag, was something she found hard to accept. Now, she wrote about how the solution to the stories she could not finish lay in harnessing the very limitations which beset her, made them hard to grasp. Rather than hiding from a literary problem, she wrote, one should foreground it, 'rail against it'.[46]

In 1972, Sontag had also been invited on a three-week trip to China. This sparked the idea for her book about China, dedicated to her father, closer to non-fiction than fiction, full of essayistic reflection and reminiscences, traveller's tales and photographs.[47] She described it to the *New Yorker* editor William Shawn as a cross between Hannah Arendt and Donald Barthelme. Instead of a book, Sontag turned this material into the story 'Project for a Trip to China', written before the China visit, which was postponed until January 1973. Susan went via North Vietnam, a month-long round trip. The journey itself was disappointing. The China of Susan's childhood dreams had little to do with the real China, as she suspected; the book about China remained in her head.

The country that formed the setting for Sontag's next major project, instead, was Israel. In October and November 1973, beginning just before the ceasefire was offically called on the Yom Kippur War, Sontag shot *Promised Lands* over five arduous, and dangerous, weeks of filming, with Nicole Stéphane as producer. It was her first 'documentary' film, yet *Promised Lands* was also personal and essayistic, even though Sontag herself did not appear in it, even as a voice – though she must have considered writing a voice-over essay – preferring to construct a collage of landscapes, streets, other voices, other views, presenting a layered and nuanced portrayal of Arab–Israeli relations (though there were no major Arab voices in it). The opening of *Promised Lands* has little dialogue for a long time, building up a poetic, impressionistic portrait through sound and images. The film is a prolonged lament, not so much for the past as for the envisioned future. Writing about making the film, Sontag averred that she wanted to 'represent a condition, rather than an action', 'a mental landscape – as well as a physical and political one'.[48] Primarily this condition was one of endlessly recurring war, two sides locked into inflexibility and bitter memory in their perception of shared rights to live in their country and have their own territory.

The process of making *Promised Lands* was refreshingly different from writing, and from the two Swedish movies. Using actors, being 'armed with a script', was utterly unlike making 'films that require plunging, unarmed, into a reality' – a reality that, as Sontag and crew went to the frontlines of the war in the Sinai Desert, included the possibility of stepping on landmines buried in the sand.[49] 'Reality was something you didn't invent', Sontag wrote. 'You ran after it, often tripping – because you were lugging a heavy tripod.'[50] The resulting film, this time, *was* an unforced improvisation, incorporating chance and accidents; as an essay-film, it also recalled the travelogues of Chris Marker.

Promised Lands brings home the reality of the war, the repetitions of history, the texture of everyday life in this bitterly contested zone. Sontag's editing of the material emphasizes themes she had explored before: the personal and sexual battle of wills in the Swedish films becomes political here. The film's final sequence is set in a military psychiatric unit: a traumatized soldier-patient is 'treated', drugged, while doctors recreate the sounds of warfare in order to trigger a reaction. This finale, continuing the psychiatric thread in Sontag's work since *Freud*, is as warped as the mind games of *Duet for Cannibals*.

While Sontag was filming in Israel, a piece by her, 'Photography', appeared in the *New York Review of Books*. This became 'In Plato's Cave', the first chapter of *On Photography*, each of whose six essays took more than six months to write. The issues in photography Sontag engaged with over the next few years would be directly nourished by the experiences she had in Israel making her documentary about war. In *Promised Lands* there were images of dead bodies, burned corpses, lying by charred tanks in the desert, as well as the sequences of shell-shocked soldiers squirming in their wards.

Sontag had filmed these images herself, and had edited them. Her moral queasiness about photography, and some of her analogies – comparing the camera to a gun, for example – were all confirmed by her own experiences as a war documentarian in the Middle East.

Before *Promised Lands*, the first inspiration for the essays on photography came when Sontag, in New York, had seen the Diane Arbus exhibition at MOMA after Arbus's death. She herself had been photographed by Arbus. Sontag subconsciously linked Arbus, who had killed herself in July 1971, with the death of Susan Taubes – and the recent demise of Alfred Chester, found dead in August 1971 in an apartment in Jerusalem after years of wandering, surrounded by empty bottles, having long since been expelled from Morocco. Was *Promised Lands* also an elegy to Alfred, a meditation on his last dwelling place? Sontag would have denied any such intention, having fallen out with Alfred years before, yet his death haunted her. Unlike Diane, Susan and Alfred, Sontag wanted to be one of the survivors, she told David.[51]

After talking with Sontag about the Arbus show, Barbara Epstein asked her if she wanted to write about it for the *New York Review of Books*. An essay ostensibly only on Arbus turned into two pieces, the first generally on photography and the second, 'Freak Show', a review of books on Arbus and Walker Evans, which appeared the following month, November 1973, also while Sontag was still filming in Israel. A further two essays on photography followed the next year, likewise initially reviews of groups of photography books. Sontag had found a subject that absorbed several of her interests, as a practising film-maker, a lover and consumer of images, an ethical theorist, surrealist and writer. *On Photography* would occupy her for some time yet. As she wrote the photography texts, she pushed them through draft after draft, as she always did with her essays; but these pages were more heavily reworked than anything she had attempted before, achieving an aphoristic density and almost fugue-like complexity.

After returning from Israel, Sontag was in New York at the end of 1973, having dinner with Elizabeth Hardwick and others; she was also in London, Milan, and Paris again. She was still seeing Nicole, regularly staying at Haramont, Nicole's house outside the city, as well as her pied-à-terre. In 1974, when Nicole would go off on Saturdays at eleven in the morning for 'the hunt',[52] not returning until after midnight, the old loneliness came flooding back to Susan, and she found herself unable to leave the rue de la Faisanderie and walk around Paris on her own. Susan often went to Venice with Nicole, staying at the Hotel Gritti, but her insecurity was not a good sign.

Early in 1975, another essay drawing from her experiences as a film-maker, 'Fascinating Fascism', on Leni Riefenstahl, appeared in the *New York Review of Books*. Sontag was in Rome in March, where she saw Carlotta again, then in Paris all summer at the rue de la Faisanderie, working away diligently – among other ongoing projects was the third novel she told several interviewers she was writing. In July, she wrote diary notes for an essay on speed, on velocity.[53] It was David Rieff who suggested that autumn that Susan should have a medical check-up. The examination revealed that she had advanced stage iv breast cancer. She was 42 years old, and was told by doctors there was only a very slim chance she would live for another two years.

6

The Kingdom of the Sick, 1975–1988

The crisis of the previous years in Sontag's writing life was now overshadowed by the diagnosis, this new and pressing crisis, sufficiently severe to demand immediate surgery. Susan, from the start, knew that she would be lucky to live. What she possibly did not know, because she was not told, is that her doctors fully expected her to die. She was admitted to Memorial Sloan-Kettering Cancer Center in New York in October, and once the doctors had a moment alone with David, they told him the bad news about his mother's chances. 'I remember pacing the corridors of the breast cancer floor at Memorial Hospital wondering what to tell my mother and what not to tell her', David writes. 'To do so seemed like sadism. But not to do so seemed like betrayal. In the end, I did nothing.'[1] David had turned 23 in September.

Susan opted for the most extreme treatment of her cancer available: a radical mastectomy in the form of a 'Halsted'. It was a brutal operation, a massive excision, removing not only her breast but muscles from the chest and lymph nodes from the armpits, followed up with 30 months of chemotherapy. Susan's arrival in what she called 'the kingdom of the sick' was abrupt, and she knew her stay there would engulf the immediate future – either ending in death or involving a long, difficult recovery, with a readjustment to her new, 'maimed' self.[2] For months after surgery, she was on tranquillizers. David could not ask her if she thought she would survive.

In her diaries, Susan wrote that she felt 'opaque to myself', hovering at the threshold between life and death. 'People speak of illness as deepening', she wrote. 'I don't feel deepened. I feel flattened.' She was in a state of 'leaky panic'. Lying in her bed in the hospital in New York, she suffered not only severe pain but acute anxiety and fear as, half knocked out by her treatment, she entered the ghostly, nightmarish hinterlands of the unwell. 'With daggers lying at the end of my dreams, I [don't] sleep much . . . I am ill, perhaps irreversibly ill.' 'Cancer = death', she wrote repeatedly in her diaries. One of the floor nurses in the hospital, swabbing Susan's dry lips, told her: 'Everyone's got to die some-time.' But, as David says, Susan 'was not ready to die at forty-two; it was as simple as that.'[3]

Once back at home in the apartment on Riverside Drive, Susan did not want to talk to David about her chances of survival. She would have to return to hospital regularly for chemotherapy for the next two and a half years. She searched for every shred of hope she could find, above all looking at new and more effective treatments. Through Nicole Stéphane's efforts, Susan heard about a doctor in Paris, Lucien Israël, an oncologist researching immuno-therapy and chemotherapy, who proposed a highly experimental treatment which was, with some persuasion, administered at Memorial Sloan-Kettering. 'Twice a week', Sontag wrote in her diary,

I return/haul myself to the hospital and present my opaque body to Doctor Green or Doctor Black, so they can tell me how I am. One pushes and pulls and pokes, admiring his handiwork, my vast scar. The other pumps me full of poison, to kill my disease but not me . . . I feel like the Vietnam War . . . they're using chemical weapons on me.[4]

The treatment was punishing. In her appearance, Susan aged rapidly, becoming prematurely old, again seeming to live her life in the wrong order. She was told she might lose all her hair. This did not happen, but she did lose some. What grew back was grey or white. She began dyeing it black, apart from a soon-to-be-distinctive silver strand. As it gradually began to become clear that Susan was surviving the treatment against the odds, she slowly regained her strength, and the vestiges of a more youthful appearance. For Sigrid Nunez, who first met Sontag in the spring of 1976, just after her surgery, and who later that year dated David, moving in to '340' with mother and son, the effect was uncanny. 'When we first met, she looked older than she would as I got to know her. As her health returned, she looked younger and younger.'[5] Nunez was unaware of the still extremely risky state of Susan's health. Susan didn't really talk about it to her. The main sign of her anxiety was her concerted attempt to stop smoking. This did not last long, however: smoking and writing were too intimately linked for Susan.

For the first months after surgery, Sontag was unable to work, too exhausted by the treatment. More than at any time in her life before, she craved company, human warmth, and spent hours on the telephone talking to friends who called to check in. As Nunez recalls, the phone rang all day. Even as Sontag slowly recovered, setting back to work on the last two essays on photography for the *New York Review of Books* in the spring and summer of 1976, she became aware that her attitude to life had fundamentally altered. The effort she needed to summon to work was enormous, but that did not bother her. It was more that the old, unthinking confidence in life had been broken. 'You can never regain that old relationship to life', Sontag reflected later.[6] She considered herself – and always would, after this sojourn in the kingdom of the sick – 'somewhat posthumous'. She felt 'very, very changed'. 'You are never the same after having undergone this terror of really facing death.'[7] There was a positive aspect to this terror, however: a giddy sense of survival, a heightening of awareness after facing such sharp edges. It was perhaps this that propelled Sontag through her creative renaissance of the next few years, with some of her most enduring books – *On Photography*, *Illness as Metaphor* and *Under the Sign of Saturn* – published swiftly after each other.

As she recovered, Sontag began to fundamentally recast the narrative she told herself about her illness, stressing the moments of elation and triumph over fate, and the drive to find the best treatment, over the bewilderment the diaries reveal she felt at the time. Part of the reweaving of this self-narrative also involved her coming to terms with her own thoughts about cancer. Initially, she had blamed herself for the illness, which she stereotypically saw as caused by a lack of passion. 'I lived as a coward, repressing my desire, my rage', Sontag wrote.[8] Meeting other cancer sufferers, she felt their shame at their illness, their stigmatization. She formulated an idea for an essay on tuberculosis and cancer, and the ways in which how people (and society) felt and talked about their illness affected their experience of it. She had two titles, 'The Discourse of Illness' and 'Illness as Metaphor', but before she began it, Sontag promised herself to finish *On Photography*.[9]

As she was getting through her illness, Sontag told Nunez she wanted 'two things: I want to work and I want to have fun'.[10] Meeting Joseph Brodsky, who was introduced to Susan in January 1976 by their mutual publisher, gave Sontag a much-needed boost while she was convalescent. Brodsky's reputation preceded him when he arrived in America as an exile from the Soviet Union. Sontag had cut out a *New York* magazine piece reprinting excerpts from his trial before she ever met him, over lunch, at a restaurant. They met again the next day.[11] Convinced of his vocation as a poet and of the exalted nature of that calling, Brodsky, 36, was also in poor physical shape, having served a year and a half of a five-year sentence for 'social parasitism' in northern Russia. He smoked heavily and had heart disease; he was missing teeth and losing his hair. 'But to Susan he was intensely romantic', Nunez writes.

Susan and Joseph embarked on an affair, which proved painfully short-lived for Susan, although their deep friendship continued. Sigrid, David, Susan and Joseph, an odd quartet, would drive around Manhattan in David's car, 'four cigarettes going, the car filled with smoke'.[12] Through Joseph, Susan became interested in poetry and Russian literature in a new way. Nicole had opened up the world of French cinema to Susan, and now Joseph did the same with Eastern European literature, an interest Susan sustained over the next decades in many essays. Joseph's experience also opened Susan's eyes to the dangers of communism, and the blinkers of many Western Marxist intellectuals, including herself. She thought of her own personal romances with Cuba, North Vietnam and China, and began to recant.

She spent the summer in Paris with Nicole, continuing to take Dr Israël's treatment. But she had yet to regain her sense of being

Joseph Brodsky in 1972.

comfortable with her body. As David has written, she never fully recovered from 'the damage done to her sexuality' by the mastectomy.[13] There were fights with Nicole that summer in Paris; in the autumn after her return to New York there was another health scare after one of Sontag's hospital check-ups revealed another operation was necessary. Nicole came to New York to stay for several weeks, and once she was gone, Carlotta came too. But Susan was as depressed as she was touched by these attentions from her ex-lovers, or soon-to-be-ex-lovers. It took until the following summer for the relationship with Nicole to collapse. After what Susan referred to in her diary as 'the last phone call from Nicole', she went into the now-familiar diary mode of self-reflection, lamentation, exhortation and crisis support. 'Let it hurt', she wrote bitterly, while also convincing herself that she had been wasting her time with Nicole the previous few years. 'I knew that.'[14] For Sigrid, the collapse of relations with Nicole meant that Susan became unbearably needy. In her loneliness, in her post-operative shock, in her fear, she was greedy for company, insatiable. 'She simply could not bear to be alone.'[15] Susan went with David and Sigrid on a Californian jaunt in the summer, then David and Susan went to Hawaii, where Mildred and Nathan Sontag had been living since the early 1970s. Sigrid was beginning to find Susan's presence stifling, and soon she moved out of '340'.

On Photography was finally published as a book towards the end of 1977. It was an immediate success. As Sontag realized when she started to tackle the Arbus exhibition, photography was still a relatively untouched subject, though she saw herself following in the footsteps of Walter Benjamin's essays on photography. It was also an infinitely interesting topic, opening out into all aspects of modernity. The six interlocking essays in *On Photography*, very carefully and even musically reworked from their original forms, laden with new aphorisms and with themes connecting from one chapter to another, made for the most coherent, unified and powerful book of critical writing Sontag had ever published.

With its essays straddling her illness, *On Photography* is a work of brooding convalescence. The writing has a new depth and gravity, with many aphorisms proving so quotable and detachable that, as Sontag would write in an essay on Walter Benjamin a year later, it feels as if 'each sentence is written as if it were the first, or the last'.[16] This in itself was an inherently photographic, Surrealist style, each sentence tempting us to take it out of context. As in Benjamin, 'something like the dread of being stopped prematurely' lay behind this compression and eloquence.[17] At any point while preparing *On Photography*, Sontag knew she might relapse and the book could remain unfinished. Her hyper-awareness of her own mortality made the themes of melancholy, death and time in photography resonate naturally.

The essays, obliquely covering the whole history of photography, allowed Sontag to enter the past, above all the nineteenth century, far more deeply than ever before. She also explored the theme of collecting for the first time at length. Behind all the aphorisms zigzagging into endlessly fragmenting argumentation, one senses Sontag herself as a curator, a collector, a lover of images. The push and pull of the essays resides in the deep allure of photography for Sontag, and her consequent moral disquiet at this allure. There is also a lovely tension in the push and pull between media, and how this book about photographs remains austerely, even abstinently, unillustrated, even as individual pictures are discussed at length. Often, we are told of a subject's gaze, the defining aesthetics of a specific photographer, yet we ourselves see nothing.

The fact that *On Photography* first arrived at its subject through Diane Arbus perhaps explains why it is so full of objections to photography: its aggression, its mercilessness, its aesthetic, ethical, interpretative problems. Arbus associated photography with transgression – 'I always thought of photography as a naughty thing to do – that was one of my favourite things about it', she wrote – and she was unfailingly attracted to the weird, the grotesque and the ugly.[18] Sontag's approach to photography is alive to its peculiarity, the distortions and transformations photography wreaks on art and reality. Sontag writes primarily as a consumer of images, not as a maker of them or a sitter for them, although she had worked as a film-maker and had sat for many well-known photographers by this point in her life. Her main angle, on the consumption of images, allows her to open out her study of photographs into a wider diagnosis of American postmodernity – one whose conclusions are hardly celebratory, gnawing away at the discordances revealed. *On Photography* was, Sontag thought, 'an extended political essay. Much more than about art. It is an extended study of our consumer world, about our experiences and the distortions by which consumerism threatens our world.'[19]

On Photography explores nearly all of Sontag's prior themes in her work: the role of art in telling us what to look at, and how to look at it, vertiginously expanded by photography; the aesthetic of quotation and fragmentation, which photography takes to an extreme; the tension between aesthetics and morality, especially in images of suffering and horror; the cannibalism of a voracious, appropriative approach to life. *On Photography* once again explores and redefines the distinctively American Surrealism that informed Sontag's earlier work. Surrealism in painting, Sontag wrote, had dwindled into a 'meagerly stocked dream world', whereas in prose fiction and photography it had come into its own. 'Photographers, operating within the terms of the Surrealist sensibility, suggest the vanity of even trying to understand the world and instead propose that we collect it.'[20] But Sontag was edging towards defining a whole new mode of consciousness, of being in the world.

Our heads are becoming like those magic boxes that Joseph Cornell filled with incongruous small objects whose provenance was a France he never once visited. Or like a hoard of old movie stills, of which Cornell amassed a vast collection in the same Surrealist spirit . . . The photographed world stands in the same, essentially inaccurate relation to the real world as stills do to movies. Life is not about significant details, illuminated in a flash, fixed forever. Photographs are.[21]

In a rare personal aside in the book, Sontag mentions the first photographic images of horror she encountered, when she was twelve, in a Santa Monica bookstore in July 1945: photographs of the Bergen-Belsen and Dachau concentration camps. 'Nothing I have seen – in photographs or in real life – ever cut me as sharply, deeply, instantaneously',[22] her sense of being 'cut' by this image surely informing Roland Barthes' distinction between the *studium* and the *punctum* in his book about photography, *Camera Lucida*, published a few years after Sontag's, in 1980. Towards the end of *On Photography*, Sontag writes at some length about China, weaving in material she gathered from her trip in 1973 but never used. Her reservations about the relatively limited and repressive Chinese ways of looking, compared to the West, offer a subtle anti-revelation, a deeply buried, self-encoded autobiographical note – a realization after so many years that her childhood obsession with China was the purest kind of myth.

Once *On Photography* was finished, Sontag began *Illness as Metaphor*, which came as quickly as the photography essays came slowly, perhaps because she had been formulating the book in her mind – and living it – since her cancer diagnosis. Sontag claimed she wrote *Illness as Metaphor* in, amazingly, a month and a half.[23] It is not a long book; indeed, like 'Trip to Hanoi' it is an extended essay, the non-fiction equivalent of a novella. Again, Sontag was propelled by the fear she might not live to finish the book; she was also filled with urgency by the desire to write something of direct practical use to other cancer sufferers. *Illness as Metaphor*, she said, was 'written in the heat of rage, fear, anguish, terror, indignation – at a time when I was very ill and my prognosis was poor'.[24] All the feelings of shame and revulsion at having cancer – and of being in some way to blame for her illness – were explored and transfigured in the writing of the book. After her diagnosis, Susan was haunted by the thought that she *deserved* her illness. Searching for new treatments, the quest for medical knowledge stripped cancer, for her, of its mythic, monolithic status, of the associations and metaphors society gave the disease. This demythologizing played a large part, she believed, in her survival.

The project of *Illness as Metaphor* was, Sontag thought, like 'Against Interpretation'.[25] It was a corrective, necessary paring back. Where tuberculosis in the nineteenth century was linked with ideas of hypersensitivity, passion and even creativity, cancer in the modern age was regarded as the disease of emotional or sexual repression, 'of the failure of expressiveness'; as 'something to conceal, and also unjust, a betrayal by one's body'.[26] There were also, Susan felt, routinely and crassly deployed military metaphors in the language surrounding cancer – and here Susan wrote in apology for her own phrase in 'What's Happening in America', 'the white race *is* the cancer of human history', which hardly gave a thought to actual cancer sufferers.[27] Of course, just as it is hard for a critic to be completely 'against interpretation', it is hard to think about illness without metaphor. Sontag begins *Illness as Metaphor* with the image of 'the kingdom of the sick', illness as 'the night-side of life': 'a brief, hectic flourish of metaphor' in order to show the allure of such thinking.[28] The image of the night-world of illness also recalls Sontag's earlier works of Freud-influenced Surrealism, and their explorations of the world of sleep, death and dreams.

Illness as Metaphor was a profoundly personal book that simply would not have been written had Sontag not been diagnosed with cancer. But Sontag deliberately avoided writing an autobiographical account of her own experience. As she put it:

I didn't think it would be useful – and I wanted to be useful –
to tell yet one more story in the first person of how someone
learned that she or he had cancer, wept, struggled, was comforted,
suffered, took courage . . . though mine was also that story.
A narrative, it seemed to me, would be less useful than an idea.
For narrative pleasure I would appeal to other writers.[29]

The long essay on illness was the closest she had ever come to
revisiting the medical and cultural territory of *Freud: The Mind
of the Moralist*, which she had written with her ex-husband all
those years ago, but now she was writing with far greater verve
and ability. What was screened out in her culturally diagnostic
approach were the details of her own journey from terror, self-
blame and confusion, towards a cure, and a new understanding
of her disease. *Illness as Metaphor* is a triumph of rationalization,
decrying the over-imaginative thoughts about disease of times
past and present; yet its certainty was only possible through
Sontag's wilful rewriting, revising what really happened to her
and how lucky she had been to survive. In her essay, she ironed
out the role of chance, of fate. Even the experimental treatment
she discovered might not have saved her. Understandably, this
was not something she liked to dwell on: she was undergoing
this very treatment as she wrote the book, part of whose role was
self-persuasion, and through self-persuasion, self-cure.

Even more so than *On Photography*, *Illness as Metaphor* moves
back into history, in its account of artistic depictions of tuberculosis
in the eighteenth and nineteenth centuries, referencing Byron and
Keats, the Goncourt brothers, Théophile Gautier, Oliver Goldsmith,
Stendhal, Henry James and Robert Louis Stevenson. As with *On
Photography*, for much of the research Sontag was now referring
from memory to her own collection of books; and the range of
allusion in *Illness as Metaphor* is wide, reaching back to the origins
of thinking about illness and melancholy. In finding portrayals of

cancer, less frequently depicted when she was writing than TB, Sontag had to try slightly harder, although she does use Tolstoy's *The Death of Ivan Ilyich*, Bernanos' *Diary of a Country Priest*, Thomas Wolfe's *Of Time and the River*, Bergman's film *Cries and Whispers* and even science fiction scenarios: *Invasion of the Body Snatchers*, *The Incredible Shrinking Man*, *The Blob* and *The Thing*.[30] She centres her discussion of cancer as a metaphor on more generally used political language and rhetoric, while also analysing the medical discourse surrounding the disease. Exposing its assumptions, Sontag writes with scorn about how cancer cells are described as 'invasive'; how they 'colonize', obliterating the body's 'defenses'; how treatment also has a military flavour, as patients during radiotherapy are 'bombarded' with toxic rays.[31]

Diagnosing attitudes towards specific illnesses, *Illness as Metaphor*, like *On Photography*, gestures towards a wider subject: the anxieties, fears and insufficiencies of the culture that spawns all these metaphors. Its deepest theme is that culture's denial of death: 'For those who live neither with religious consolations about death nor with a sense of death (or anything else) as natural, death is the obscene mystery, the ultimate affront, the thing that cannot be controlled. It can only be denied.'[32] *Illness as Metaphor*, like *Death Kit*, was another ode on mortality, this time written in the glare of imminent extinction. As with many of Sontag's most striking statements, she is also writing from a coded personal standpoint – referring to her own denial of death since the death of her father. Her long essay's very practicality, however, colluded in the denial of death again, even as it faces it: it would read very differently, with an undertow of pathos rather than of victory, if Sontag had not survived. Yet, against the odds, she *was* miracu-lously surviving, determined to hold on to life.

At the end of 1977 as she was finishing *Illness as Metaphor*, Susan travelled to Venice with Joseph Brodsky for the Biennale, the theme of which that year was 'dissent', primarily in those socialist

European countries silencing their intellectuals. She arrived on a clear day in early December, meeting Alberto Moravia at the airport and finding Venice looking more beautiful than ever. Joseph gave an evening reading at the Teatro Ateneo, which enthralled Susan. In Venice Susan also saw György Konrád, the Hungarian writer, who, Susan thought, looked uncannily like Jacob Taubes; at breakfast with Konrád she discovered that Susan Taubes had an affair with him in Budapest in August 1969. Susan oscillated, in her diaries, between thoughts on censorship and writers' freedoms, provoked by the Biennale, and lyrical travel notes, bewitched by the city in the winter fog and snow. Walking at night through Venice was enchanting: 'so much beauty. Like breathing pure oxygen.' The creaking of the vaporetto piers in the water, gulls cooing, the view of the basilica at night, all thrilled her.[33]

Back in New York, the lease on '340' had run out. Susan and David had to find another place to live in the spring, moving to a duplex on East 17th Street.[34] *Illness as Metaphor* was published over the summer, after being serialized in instalments in the NYRB. Perhaps because Susan was becoming more free of her illness – according to her doctors, there was 'considerable optimism'[35] by this stage – she did a lot of travelling that summer, to Madrid, Venice again, Paris, London and the Bayreuth Festival. The flurry of post-illness publications continued with Sontag's collection of stories, *I, Etcetera*, coming out that winter.

The collection, so named as Sontag saw it as 'a series of adventures with the first person' (and also another nod to Alfred Chester with his novel *I, Etc.*), was a very mixed bag, of variable quality, containing work dating back to the early 1960s alongside recent stories.[36] 'Old Complaints Revisited', a tale of a dissatisfied translator for a massive bureaucracy, was a reworking of material from an abandoned science fiction project, pre-*Death Kit*, called 'The Organization'. 'The Dummy', a story of a man who creates a double to live his life for him, was published in *Harper's* in 1963.

'American Spirits' appeared in *Partisan Review* in 1965.[37] It is the later stories in *I, Etcetera* – 'Project for a Trip to China', 'Debriefing' and 'Unguided Tour' – all more profoundly autobiographical, which carry the collection and whose experimental styles work best when harnessed to a fund of emotion. These three stories drew on Sontag's childhood, her friendship with Susan Taubes, and her lifelong love of travel, respectively, creating an entirely original, fast, nervy, perspective-shifting, notebook-like yet also moving, luscious style.

After the launch of *I, Etcetera* in November 1978, Sontag was again in Italy, musing on the beauty of Venice in the winter. She had been rereading Henry James's *The Golden Bowl*. All her gathered impressions of the city, which now carried memories of love affairs – with Irene, Carlotta, Nicole and Joseph – made it easy for her to choose, when asked to make a film for Italian television as part of a series on cities, what she would portray. *Unguided Tour*, based on Susan's story in *I, Etcetera*, was not made for a few years, but that December, Susan's diary notes were strongly visual, as she saw Venice almost as a photographic negative of how it appeared in summer.

She continued to travel relentlessly, to the familiar European points of her compass. In the spring of 1979 she went to California on her way to Tokyo for a three-week lecture tour. She was now planning a book about Japan, which, like the China project, never materialized, though she continued to visit Japan in later years.[38] That summer and autumn Sontag also embarked on her first production of a play as a director, Luigi Pirandello's *As You Desire Me*, in Italy. Adriana Asti had again agreed to star. Sontag made Pirandello's play her own, bringing out its latent themes of 'psychological cannibalism', as well as photography.[39] Acting, she discovered, was 'physical work'.[40] Unlike her films, she found the play ultimately belonged not to the director but to the actors, who ensured it was different in every performance. By the end of its run, *As You Desire Me* was completely and potently changed.

Returning to New York, Sontag was working on the final essays for *Under the Sign of Saturn* and dreaming up future topics in her diaries, including an essay on aphorisms, fragments and notebooks, which she saw as part of her constantly announced farewell to essay writing. She was also thinking about ideas for fiction, for stories, as well as her third novel, likewise constantly announced. In May 1980 she went on an organized trip to Poland with a group of American writers including Joyce Carol Oates and John Ashbery. Sontag was herself partly Polish, and so the trip was a kind of homecoming. She visited Warsaw and Krakow, and vowed to come back to Poland again, next time on her own.

Under the Sign of Saturn, a collection of seven essays from the 1970s, was published in autumn 1980, dedicated to Joseph Brodsky. Over these years Sontag's essayistic voice had become – and this process continued – more personal, less idea-driven, more humane. She called the pieces in *Under the Sign of Saturn* 'portraits of consciousness' and thought they were closer in style to her fiction.[41] The volume is more purely literary than her previous collections – five of the seven pieces, on Paul Goodman, Antonin Artaud, Walter Benjamin, Roland Barthes and Elias Canetti, are on writers. It is also unusual for her in its being primarily a series of studies of individuals. Even the two pieces on film and photography, 'Fascinating Fascism' and 'Syberberg's Hitler', focus on single figures. This individual focus lends the collection a greater psychological depth than before.

The seven portraits in the book are all, to differing degrees, portraits of the saturnine temperament. They are all suffused with melancholy and restlessness. The monumental essay on Artaud is the most extreme and disaffected, and the essay on Riefenstahl the most severely critical of its subject, as Sontag revokes her earlier claim in 'On Style', from *Against Interpretation*, that Riefenstahl's Nazi affiliations did not deny the artistic mastery of her films. (Now, in a complete reversal, Sontag writes of Riefenstahl's *Triumph of the Will* as 'a film whose very conception negates the possibility of the filmmaker's having an aesthetic conception independent of propaganda'.[42]) Several of the essays, in admiring writers, are *about* admiration, with Sontag also noting how Benjamin, Barthes and Canetti wrote criticism that was also self-portraiture. In just the same way, the admiring portraits of *Under the Sign of Saturn* also form a self-portrait of Sontag, in her forties, also a lifelong admirer, sharer of passions, and melancholic.

In her diaries, Sontag thought the best review of the collection would be an eighth essay depicting herself in the same way that she portrayed them,[43] delineating the pathos of avidity, of collecting and of melancholy in her own case, and the impossibility of the intellectual project. The ending of the Canetti essay is a seemingly self-directed assessment of the ideal role of admiration. It could be read as Sontag's own view of the limitations of criticism, and her attempt to transcend her own intellectual energy; her inability to breathe deeply, artistically or personally, as the 1980s began.

Her personal fear of loneliness was mirrored by her need for artistic nourishment, which found such a fertile, instructive and lucid outlet in her essays. Critically, she was also a vampire, a cannibal, feeding constantly on new work, finding new things to admire; her awareness of this need was why she so disliked her own criticism and constantly vowed to give it up. In the lifelong oscillation in her work between purity and silence, and wisdom and accumulation, she placed a higher value on the former qualities while tending more naturally towards the latter. The religious, devotional aspect of Sontag's work, which had been there ever since she studied religion at Harvard, meant that she always saw her cannibalistic, hungry side as tainted. She always wanted to transcend her own avidity, or to transform it into something else, as she wrote at the close of the Canetti piece:

The last achievement of the serious admirer is to stop immediately putting to work the energies aroused by, filling up the space opened by, what is admired. Thereby talented admirers give themselves permission to breathe, to breathe more deeply. But for that it is necessary to go beyond avidity; to identify with something beyond achievement, beyond the gathering of power.[44]

After *Under the Sign of Saturn*, Sontag felt she had 'discharged my debts to my own obsessions. A tremendous liberation.' Perhaps she thought, or hoped, that she would write – or need to write – fewer essays from now on, turning instead back to fiction. She continued, of course, to write essays throughout the early 1980s: they answered to such a craving in her that she would never be able to abstain entirely. Yet by early 1981 Sontag was deep into writing a novel, 'a long, complex book' with several narrators. By 1983, she had also begun a novella set in the 1920s.[45] This last, it appears, was about a dancer, loosely based on Isadora Duncan.[46]

Neither was ever finished. In her own diagnosis, part of the problem with the long novel was that she kept on leaving it to do other things – direct the Pirandello play or write essays – and by the time she returned to it her concentration had been lost.[47] With the novella, perhaps she had not yet quite overcome her antipathy to period novels. But her fictional aspirations throughout the 1980s remained buoyant, centred on the manuscript which began to take the name 'The Western Half', about Polish and Soviet émigrés in America, one of whose central figures was based on Joseph Brodsky.[48] She continued to work on the manuscript until nearly the end of the decade before finally abandoning it. But this theme of émigrés was to be redeemed with her final novel, *In America*, which transmuted it into the past.

Peggy Jarrell
Kaplan, *Lucinda
Childs*, 1984.

The essays of the early 1980s, like the novella, also often
touched on the subject of dance. And much of Susan's essayistic
interest in dance focused on a single figure, Lucinda Childs, with
whom Susan became fascinated, and involved. Childs, who was
seven years younger than Susan, born in 1940, studied with Merce
Cunningham, was connected with the experimental Judson Dance
Theater in the 1960s and formed her own dance company in the
1970s. Like Susan, she also sat for Warhol's *Screen Tests* in the
1960s, very likely on the same day that Warhol shot his film of the
Village Voice dance critic, *Jill Johnston Dancing* (1963).[49] In her *Screen
Tests*, Childs, in her twenties, is determined, combative, intense,
wary. Her breakthrough came with her collaboration with Robert
Wilson and Philip Glass on the opera *Einstein on the Beach*, which
premiered in France in 1976 and toured across Europe before a very
short showing – two Sundays at the Metropolitan Opera – in
New York. The experience of preparing and touring *Einstein* was

a pivotal year for Childs, and encouraged her to stage the first of her large-scale works, *Dance*, in 1979, with music again by Glass, and a film by Sol LeWitt. Susan had seen *Einstein on the Beach* and made a brief note about it in her diaries in early 1977; a regular for years at the Met, she did not share Joseph Brodsky's dismissive view of dance.[50]

Susan was at the opening of Childs's third large-scale production, *Available Light*, first presented at the Châteauvallon dance festival in 1983. She was writing a detailed, ludic essay about the development of Childs's aesthetic, 'A Lexicon for *Available Light*', tracing the move from Childs's anti-traditional beginnings to an almost neoclassical postmodernism (a term Sontag always resisted) or minimalism: an art of Apollonian grace, symmetry, purity. Writing about dance, for Sontag, was a development of the interests she had explored in 'The Aesthetics of Silence' and *Brother Carl*: she found something cleansing, unattainable, even spiritual in dance, which shifted her aesthetics on to a different axis.

In 1982, when she finally made her film about Venice, *Unguided Tour*, for Italian TV, Lucinda Childs was the female star, alongside an Italian actor, Claudio Cassinelli. Sontag and Childs were in Venice in October that year shooting the film, which was edited for three months in Rome. *Unguided Tour*, or *Letter from Venice*, an elliptical dialogue between two unhappy lovers on the verge of breaking up, was layered with Susan's own experiences. She thought it was the best of her films. Years of visiting Venice, brooding on the melancholy spirit of the city, and her own inter-woven memories, saturated and informed its themes. In her diaries, Sontag made a list of all the trips to Venice she had made with different lovers.[51] It would always be a palimpsestic centre of her romantic imagination, of her own past.

If in one way her work was becoming more abstract and poetic, it was also retaining, at the other extreme, a deeply political, public, hard-hitting edge. Earlier in 1982 in New York, Sontag had been involved in a tense fracas over her speech at a rally for Polish Solidarity at Town Hall, in which she made her notorious, provocative declaration – 'Communism is in itself a variant, the most successful variant, of fascism. Fascism with a human face' – to catcalls, booing and uproar from the audience, and an ensuing torrent of hostile comment in the American press.[52] Sontag told the writer Edmund White in advance of the event that she knew the speech would not go down well.[53]

She was also writing a long essay (which she eventually gave up) throughout the early 1980s on communism and Western intellectuals, called 'Before the Revolution', beginning with André Gide's trip to Russia in 1936.[54] She spent a year and a half on the jettisoned communism essay, writing hundreds of pages before bailing out.[55] She also spent over six months on an essay on Sartre for the *New York Review of Books*, titled 'Sartre's Abdication', an 'anti-self-portrait', likewise abandoned.[56] Even essay writing was slipping out of her grasp, though she continued to write interesting pieces – on Balanchine, on Proust, on the actress Veruschka.[57] With age, the essays were getting harder to write, partly because Sontag was struggling with their autobiographical element, which she now wanted to emphasize. She wanted to weave herself more directly into her essays, using the first person. But this was antithetical to her earlier style, and the adjustment was not easy.

Her publishers issued *A Susan Sontag Reader* around this time, a collection of her work, which intensified her feeling of being posthumous since her cancer. She made a television documentary on the dancer Pina Bausch, and after that directed a stage adaptation of Diderot by Milan Kundera, *Jacques and His Master*, at Harvard. She became increasingly involved with International PEN, and would eventually become president of PEN in 1987, championing many international literary and political causes, including prominently supporting Salman Rushdie after the fatwa – all part of what she later called 'her "Girl-Scout-ish" obsession with doing "worthy" things'.[58] More and more, as Sontag grew older, she could be roused into battle for any number of different causes, and something deep within her relished high-profile verbal combat, no matter how bloody it became. Her nerves for any sort of public controversy grew to be very strong.

But, as she entered her fifties, Sontag found that her melancholy and loneliness began to become more intense. She also felt physically exhausted, and was having problems concentrating. Sigrid Nunez, who split up with David years earlier, still saw Susan sometimes. Nunez writes of this period that Susan's 'chronic irritability and discontent shaded into something darker. She found herself crawling back into bed soon after getting up.' Susan saw a neurologist who told her she was suffering clinical depression, at midlife. 'Always when I saw her now she complained of being lonely, of feeling rejected, abandoned. Sometimes she wept', Nunez writes.[59]

Some of her writing around this period is reflective, autobiographical, charged with loneliness. In her story 'The Letter Scene', published in the *New Yorker* in 1986, Susan wove in small, piercing fragments of autobiography that dealt with her marriage to Philip. The year after the divorce, she awoke most days with a smile on her face, she wrote. But she never again experienced such intimacy, and she wrote nostalgically of how they never stopped talking during the marriage, even following each other into the bathroom. 'I've never felt so safe with anyone since', Sontag wrote, at a distance of several decades:

> It's not right to feel so safe. I don't, I can't, reread his letters. But I need to think of them there, in the shoebox, in the bottom of my closet. They are part of my life, my dead life.[60]

Some of her need for intimacy had been transferred to David. Nunez writes that Susan's therapist had asked her at one point, 'Why did you try to make a father out of your son?' At first Susan

Sontag, photographed by Sophie Bassouls in 1983.

was aghast at this. 'But then it hit her,' Susan told Nunez: 'she *had* tried to do that. And we both started to cry.'[61]

HIV and AIDS were beginning to claim many of Sontag's friends. The liberation of the gay community in New York in the 1970s turned into illness and mourning in the 1980s, as one person after another contracted the disease. Acquaintances, friends of friends, and close friends of Sontag, in an ever-expanding chain, began to fall ill, and die. One day in 1986, Sontag received a phone call telling her that Joe Chaikin had AIDS. She cried when she hung up, then, unable to sleep, took a bath. The opening of the story 'The Way We Live Now' came to her. 'I got out of the bathtub and started writing standing up', Sontag said. 'I wrote the story very quickly, drawing on experiences of my own cancer and a friend's stroke.'[62] The stroke was Joseph Brodsky's – he had been in and out of hospital, for his heart, ever since they met. Susan went to visit Chaikin, who was eventually unable to speak as the illness took hold, nearly every day in the hospital. Soon, other friends were affected, including Paul Thek, whom Susan also visited regularly and who died in August 1988. The sickbed was once again a central part of Susan's life.

'The Way We Live Now', arising from these circumstances, is a short masterpiece. It has 26 narrators, one for each letter of the alphabet. Their reported conversations and comments, focusing on a sick person they know (although the specific illness is never mentioned), are threaded into a continuous stream of neurotic, perfectly inflected, chatty New York prose, as if tapping into a series of telephone conversations. Sontag had never before captured this tone in her writing, so seemingly close to the intimate speech of her Manhattan friends. The story is also deeply moving, drawing so obviously on Susan's reliving of her cancer diagnosis of a decade before, when she and her network of friends were likewise so anxiously facing death. Now, vicariously, she was back in the kingdom of the sick, and it was a subject she wrote about with earned authority. The long, run-on lines of the story perfectly capture the queasy, drugged, heightened, fearful reality of illness, of living on 'the night-side of life', though it is not the patient who speaks, but all his friends. The Chinese Whispers form matches the disease, which links everyone in a new way, changing sexuality and the way we live now, for 'everyone is at risk, everyone who has a sexual life, because sexuality is a chain that links each of us to many others, unknown others, and now the great chain of being has become a chain of death as well'.[63]

Sontag collaborated with the artist Howard Hodgkin on the story, and Hodgkin worked for several years on a series of abstract, lush, glowing, weirdly sinister and virulent hand-tinted colour etchings, incorporated into the book, *The Way We Live Now*, published in 1991, five years after it first appeared in the *New Yorker*.[64] Sontag had been – and would continue to be – criticized throughout her career by the gay community, for not coming out publicly as bisexual. But her work repeatedly engaged, from *The Benefactor* and 'Notes on "Camp"' onwards, with gay culture; and *The Way We Live Now* also responded artistically to the crisis in her community. She was a non-joiner. She wanted to be seen as a writer, not a gay activist, a feminist, a postmodernist or suchlike. But with her privacy about her bisexuality there was also an element of self-protection, going back to when she had fought in court for custody of David after her divorce. She knew she had plenty to lose from being publicly 'outed' – not least, David.

There were more deaths in the mid-1980s. In December 1986, Mildred Sontag died from lung cancer in Hawaii. Nat Sontag died a year later.[65] Susan was in Hawaii, serving on the jury of the film festival there that year, when Mildred was taken ill. Perhaps in response to her mother's death, Susan began to work on the memoir that became 'Pilgrimage'. She was also at work on a non-fiction response to AIDS, the book-length essay *AIDS and Its*

Metaphors, which dealt with the AIDS crisis very differently. Sontag
began the piece as a short epilogue to a new edition of *Illness as
Metaphor*; yet the subject grew into something more substantial.
In the end it became a sequel to the earlier book on illness,
revisiting and updating its themes in light of the new epidemic.
Where the counterpart to cancer had been tuberculosis, here
Sontag drew on comparisons with syphilis. AIDS, she wrote, was
seen metaphorically as a plague; the feeling of shame that fell
on so many cancer sufferers was worse with AIDS: there was
'an imputation of guilt' due to the transmission of the HIV virus
through sex and drug use.[66]

Written during the ongoing crisis of the virus in New York, the
AIDS essay is more reportorial and objective than the cancer book;
it also lacks the depth of its personal momentum. The sense of
restrained feeling, of melancholy, which informs 'The Way We Live
Now' and the cancer and photography essays, is not fully present in
the essay on AIDS, which strains to make its arguments persuasive.
Where the understated autobiographical subtext of *Illness as
Metaphor* – Sontag's own illness as a cancer patient – made that
essay all the more powerful, the unstated autobiographical subtext
of *AIDS and Its Metaphors* – Sontag's own experience as a bisexual
– made her text on AIDS look strangely limp and coy. This was
perhaps why the book drew such fire from its critics, especially
from the gay community.

However, *AIDS and Its Metaphors* did have one transforming,
coincidental effect on Susan's own life. During publicity sessions
for the book in 1988, Susan was photographed by Annie Leibovitz.
It was the first time they had met, and they also went out to dinner
together, where Leibovitz asked Sontag, among other things, about
The Benefactor. Leibovitz was 39, Sontag 55. It was the beginning of
a passionate relationship between photographer and subject which
would continue, on and off, for the next sixteen years. This was
longer than Sontag spent with Philip, with Irene, with Nicole, with

Joseph. The relationship with Annie, much as David called it an 'on-again, off-again' affair,[67] would become the longest-running love of Sontag's life, which over the next few years began to have more fulfilment.

7

Beginning Again, 1988–2000

Sontag had never had such a serious relationship with a photographer before, though she had been friends with many photographers, even before she wrote *On Photography*. She had been photographed by Diane Arbus, Peter Hujar and Robert Mapplethorpe, among others, and knew them all personally to some degree. These were fast becoming historical figures: after Arbus's suicide there was wide interest in her work; Hujar died of complications from AIDS in 1987, as would Mapplethorpe in 1989. Annie Leibovitz had also been photographed by Mapplethorpe, appearing in his book *Certain People: A Book of Portraits* (1985), in which Sontag likewise featured and for which she wrote the preface, mainly about the discomfort she felt being photographed. Sontag was thus intensely aware of Leibovitz when they first met for the session for *AIDS and Its Metaphors*, just as Leibovitz was intensely aware of who Sontag was. The relationship between photographer and subject was also a relationship between a practitioner and a theorist. Sontag relished her advisory, nurturing role towards Leibovitz, who also nurtured her creatively.

Leibovitz, born in 1949, had studied at the San Francisco Art Institute in the late 1960s before beginning her career working as a rock and roll photographer for *Rolling Stone* throughout the 1970s and early '80s, going on tour with many of the bands she photographed and, in an extraordinary, grisly coincidence, taking an iconic photo of John Lennon and Yoko Ono just hours before

Lennon was shot in 1980. She moved to *Vanity Fair* in 1983 and became more of a portrait photographer, making her first studio portraits in the 1980s in a large space on Vandam Street in New York and becoming hugely in demand as a celebrity portraitist. Yet she was not entirely comfortable with studio portraiture, despite her success, and when she met Sontag, Leibovitz claims, she was unsure of her direction. 'I'd always had this edge. I was the bad girl coming from the rock and roll magazine, and the edge was sort of peeling away.' Sontag 'told me she thought I could be good'.[1] Leibovitz came from a large, loving family, the third child of six, and spent her early years moving around, as her father worked for the u.s. Air Force, often being transferred from one base to another. She shared Sontag's Jewish background, but not the sense of dislocation from her roots. Her father had grown up in Connecticut, meeting her mother during the Second World War; they settled in Maryland after retirement. He 'lived for our family', Leibovitz writes.[2] She also remained close to her brothers and sisters.

If Leibovitz was less than sure of herself as a photographer when the two met, Sontag was also at a low ebb as a writer, after all the unfinished projects of the 1980s, her least productive decade. She was also struggling financially a little. She was now living in an apartment in a town house on King Street, where the rent was far greater than in the days of '340'. In a story she told and retold to interviewers, Sontag woke up one night in the King Street apartment to find her bedroom on fire. She escaped unhurt, but what shocked her afterwards was the realization she could not afford to spend the night in a hotel.[3] She had never been overly concerned with money as a writer, making just enough through her books and the occasional talk or lecture – although during her illness in the 1970s, her lack of health insurance meant she could not pay her medical bills. (Robert Silvers of the *New York Review of Books* raised $150,000 for her.) Writing was a vocation for Sontag, not a commercial enterprise. She was making far less than many of her

Robert Mapplethorpe, *Annie Leibovitz*, 1983.

friends, and she was now in her late fifties. All of this lay behind her decision to engage an agent for the first time. The move was effective: in early 1989, through Andrew Wylie, Sontag signed a large, four-book deal with her usual publishers, Farrar, Straus & Giroux. The following year, she was awarded a huge five-year MacArthur Fellowship.

For the first time in her life Sontag was financially secure; and in love again. She went to Mexico and Venice with Leibovitz in 1989, staying at the Gritti Palace in Venice – that haunt of so many old romances. That September, Sontag moved to Berlin in order to begin work on a new novel. This was *The Volcano Lover*, which she continued to write over the next three years, a period when she abstained more than ever before from writing essays, perhaps encouraged by Leibovitz to call a halt, as Sontag always said she wanted to do, to writing criticism. Later, Sontag would portray the composition of *The Volcano Lover* – her first published novel for 25 years – as a miraculous opening of the creative floodgates, a tremendous emotional release, a wondrous beginning again, after years of stalling. 'I fell into the book like Alice in Wonderland', she said. 'For three years, I worked 12 hours a day in a delirium of pleasure.'[4] 'The whole novel was a discovery of furious permissions I granted myself.'[5]

Sontag had chosen to live in Berlin as it provided a 'double distancing'[6] which generally worked in her favour when she was writing abroad: she was not in New York, nor in the place she was writing about (Italy). Between the autumn of 1989 and the end of 1990, she wrote half of *The Volcano Lover*, mainly in Berlin. Publication of the novel was still some way off, however. Sontag also became a playwright around this time, penning her play *Alice in Bed* in Berlin, in two weeks in January 1990; it premiered in Bonn the following year. And this was not Sontag's only play: her radically condensed version of Wagner's *Parsifal*, a very short script called *A Parsifal*, written in lieu of a catalogue essay for an exhibition of the work of Robert Wilson at the Museum of Fine Arts in Boston, appeared in 1991.[7]

A Parsifal is a *jeu d'esprit* in the spirit of Gertrude Stein, a surrealist essay in play form (with an ostrich as one central figure in the drama), which worries away quizzically at problems of spectatorship, suffering and inaction in war that would continue to concern Sontag over the next decade. It was not produced in Sontag's lifetime, but it opened up to her the possibilities of writing in dramatic form, which she had not previously done for the stage rather than the screen, despite her experiences as a theatre director and her interest in theatre as a critic.

Alice in Bed was much longer, with eight scenes, but it was also essentially essayistic in conception, constructed around the static discussion of ideas rather than outright drama. Sontag had the idea for *Alice in Bed* while directing Adriana Asti in her Pirandello production a decade earlier. Asti had declared she wanted Sontag to write a play for her in which she would remain on stage throughout. Sontag had joked that in order to do that, she would have to stay in bed. Sontag immediately thought of doing a play about Alice James, the brilliant sister of Henry and William James – but it took her ten years to get around to writing it.

Set in London in 1890, with a brief flashback to the James family home in Cambridge, Massachusetts, decades earlier, *Alice in Bed* was 'a free fantasy'[8] based on the thwarted life of Alice James who, unable to find an outlet for her evident genius (other than her private diaries), spent all of her adult life as an invalid, suffering from obscure ailments until – in an obvious parallel to Sontag's own life – she was diagnosed with breast cancer aged 43. Where Sontag had survived, Alice died, falling into death in a swoon. In the eight scenes of the play, Sontag explores Alice's helplessness, and the 'grief and anger of women'[9] evoked by her bedridden state, as Alice talks with successive people: her nurse; her father, who absent-mindedly gives her permission to commit suicide; her brother Henry; the ghostly kindred spirits Emily Dickinson, Margaret Fuller, Myrtha from *Giselle*, Kundry from *A Parsifal*, Alice's dead mother; and a cockney burglar who enters her room.

Conflating Alice James's life with another Alice, that of Lewis Carroll, Sontag stages a mad tea party in the middle of the play in which Alice smokes opium with her ghostly visitors. Despite the real historical figures, and the anguish of the plight of Victorian women, the play floats free of reality: a hallucinatory, surreal atmosphere swirls around Alice's sickbed, and events take place largely in her mind. The play revisits the world of *Illness as Metaphor*, but in a surprisingly light and comic way, full of absurd laughs and witty dialogue; more tragically, it also revisits the world of *Death Kit*, in that Alice's lifelong invalidism is a kind of prolonged suicide. As in *Death Kit*, there is also a journey in *Alice in Bed*, in Alice's long monologue in scene six, on how she can 'travel with my mind' to Rome and Italy:

> The views push on, one view translates into another, there are walls, doors, arches, terraces, another view, another change, but it's still the same place: Rome – in my mind. I can go as far as I want, I can do what I can't do, what I shouldn't do, in my mind.[10]

The imagination is exalting, and the only escape for a woman who, as her brother Henry says, found in her 'tragic health . . . the only solution . . . of the problem of life – as it suppressed the lament of equality, reciprocity, etc.' But, as Sontag writes in her note on the play, 'the victories of the imagination are not enough.'[11] In its tracing of the limits of the imagination and the world entirely in the mind, the play also revisits *The Benefactor*. Sontag's own wilfulness, her refusal to be defeated by life, her strength, her compulsion to pay attention to the wider world outside, mean she cannot endorse Alice's helpless state, even as Alice's life of the mind is also the life of a writer. The play traces the very real limits of Alice's state as a woman who cannot fully define herself in her society. Yet Sontag's Alice can't get up because she won't, just as much as she won't because she can't. The play is also Sontag's first successfully finished attempt at writing a story set in the past with real figures. The freedom and wit Sontag brought to the project of dramatizing Alice James's anxiously confined hypochondriac life was also brought to the book she was immersed in writing, which played fast and loose – although not to such a radical extent as the play – with the conventions of the historical novel.

Returning from Berlin to New York early in 1991 to continue writing *The Volcano Lover*, Sontag found a new apartment. Now she had more money, she installed herself more grandly, in a five-room penthouse in Chelsea, in London Terrace, where Leibovitz also lived – the two each had a view of the other's place. Sontag's address was West 24th Street, Leibovitz's West 23rd. From her terrace balcony, Sontag once again had a view of the Hudson, as she had at '340'. She set up a library for her collection of books, which had now swelled to a considerable size, with shelves reaching up to the ceiling. As she worked on *The Volcano Lover*, with her new assistant Karla Eoff, she sat in the middle of a large room full of books, with Eoff typing up Sontag's handwritten drafts, at first using Sontag's Selectric, before she finally bought a computer. In the later stages of the compositional process, Sontag dictated her drafts straight to Eoff, correcting and editing as she went along.

Most of *The Volcano Lover* was written in Berlin and the Chelsea apartment, but there was also a two-week stint in a hotel in Milan in 1991, with another pivotal chapter – the deathbed monologue of a central character, the Cavaliere – written in three days after Sontag checked herself in to the Mayflower Hotel in New York to work on it.[12] Sontag also visited some of the sites in the novel for research; she even climbed Mount Vesuvius, one of the book's central presences. When the time came to revise the proofs, Sontag and Eoff holed up for a week in the London Terrace apartment without going out, working and reworking the text.[13]

The Volcano Lover was a completely new start for Sontag, an artistic re-beginning in her late fifties that involved working within a new genre (the historical novel), and different ways of researching and writing. Her evolution as a novelist depended on a paradoxical unlearning of ideas and techniques: while *The Benefactor* and *Death Kit* played avant-garde games with narrative and reality, *The Volcano Lover* was closer to older, traditional forms of the novel, and would probably have seemed as regressive to the young Sontag as her 1960s *nouveau roman*-ish experiments now seemed dry and solipsistic to her older self. Her work had been growing in its grasp of history and the past, and gaining greatly from this depth. She had now also learned, as a writer, the importance of sensory detail. While working on her memoir 'Pilgrimage' in the 1980s, Sontag told Sigrid Nunez that she didn't notice details in the way that, say, Nabokov did; or she later forgot what she did notice. Writing 'Pilgrimage', for example, 'she could remember almost nothing specific about Thomas Mann's house that day. Which was very frustrating, she said, now that she wanted to tell that story.'[14] Writing *The Volcano Lover*, Sontag learned to linger over details with a care she had never applied to fiction before. And she learned to incorporate essayistic flourishes and aphorisms into storytelling more naturally, while also making the book into a distinctively postmodern, knowing take on the historical novel.

The idea for *The Volcano Lover* had been germinating for over a decade, after Sontag's discovery of some engravings of Mount Vesuvius in a book and print shop near the British Museum on a visit to London in the early 1980s. The engravings had been commissioned by Sir William Hamilton, the British ambassador

Pietro Fabris after William Hamilton, 'The Crater of Mount Vesuvius', print after a drawing, in Hamilton's *Campi Phlegrai: Observations of the Volcanoes of the Two Sicilies* (1779).

to Naples, in 1776. Sontag's initial idea was to write a text about the engravings for the Italian magazine *FMR*.[15] As she found out more about Hamilton – whose life had been dramatized in the film *That Hamilton Woman* (1941, dir. Alexander Korda) and in one biography from 1969, by Brian Fothergill – the shape of a polyphonic, epic novel slowly formed in Sontag's mind. She sympathized with Hamilton's melancholic temper, his connoisseurship, his passion for collecting, all of which matched traits of her own. She learned about his first marriage, to Catherine Barlow, which ended with her death, and his subsequent infatuation with and marriage in 1791 to the much younger (by 36 years) Emma Lyon, later called Emma Hart and finally Lady Emma Hamilton. Emma was a painter's model, an actress, a beauty, who sat for George Romney and Sir Joshua Reynolds, and who performed 'attitudes' – an art of miming and impersonating famous people. After marrying Hamilton, Emma fell in love with Lord Nelson, beginning a *ménage à trois* that is at the dramatic core of Sontag's novel, which climaxes with the eruption of Vesuvius in 1794 and the bloodthirsty French revolutionary Terror reaching Naples.

Sontag had always been slightly wary of historical novels, and even later, once she herself was a full-fledged historical novelist, she noted in an essay on Anna Banti's *Artemisia*, which ultimately praised the genre, how 'stories that take place in the past are often assumed to be old-fashioned in form and concern. The very fact of being concerned with the past is taken to be an evasion or an escape from the present.'[16] Part of Sontag's suspicion lay in her deep instinct for artistic currency, and her sense of the artist's role being to direct attention and perception. In history, so many potential subjects cried out for treatment that it was hard to know where in particular to find significance for the present. *The Volcano Lover* begins with the figure of the author herself, scouting for a story to tell in the labyrinthine precincts of the past; Sontag opens with an account of herself at a flea market in Manhattan in the spring of 1992, 'in my jeans and silk blouse and tennis shoes' searching for 'something that speaks to me'.[17]

The main focus for *The Volcano Lover*, initially, was the slightly desiccated, discerning figure of William Hamilton; yet Sontag also gives as much of herself to her portrayal of Emma, who steals the show in the second half of the novel. William, the Cavaliere, 'ferried himself past one vortex of melancholy after another by means of an astonishing spread of enthusiasms. He is interested in everything.' His collecting, like Sontag's, is avid, insatiable. He even collects Emma: 'it did not matter if she loved him, so much did he love her, love watching her.' She is 'the proud possession, publicly displayed, of a great collector'. Emma, like Sontag in her essays, borrows styles and masks, always having 'a pretext for performing . . . reproducing the postures and demeanour of some figure of history or poetry'.[18] Sontag, like Emma, had also been an artist's model, having sat for so many photographers. Self-made, much admired, vivacious, Emma suffers for being a woman, is discredited in some deep way for her beauty.

In *The Volcano Lover* Sontag depicted her main characters with far more passion than ever before in her fiction. Her prose was voluptuous, arch, elegant, with a satisfying tang of eighteenth-century wit. Sontag spoke of writing the novel in a language of licentiousness, in terms of 'permissions' and 'pleasure'; she even said the novel opened out for her one day in conversation with her analyst, who asked her, '"What makes you think it isn't a contribution to give people pleasure?" . . . "And I thought, ohhhhhh. That sentence launched me."'[19] Alongside the depth of the characterization – and without undermining this depth – a significant part of this narrative pleasure, for the reader, lies in *The Volcano Lover*'s subversion of the historical novel, and how we are always dimly aware of Sontag's presence as a late twentieth-century creator behind her antique figures, whom we nonetheless feel for. The novel is poised between emotional identification and distance in a very original and

John Jones after George Romney (*c.* 1872–94), *Emma Hamilton,* *c.* 1901, lithograph.

sophisticated way. The narrative is also laced with quintessentially Sontagian aphorisms, above all on collecting – enough, if extracted, to make a short volume on the subject – and meditations on depicting suffering, above all the differences in the practice of doing so between the eighteenth and late twentieth centuries. The novel becomes extremely gory once the Revolution takes over in Naples, but the meditative thread on suffering distances us from the violence and comments on the moral problematics of this distance, pointing back to *On Photography* and forward to *Regarding the Pain of Others.*

What people admired then was an art (whose model was the classical one) that minimized the pain of pain. It showed people able to maintain decorum and composure, even in monumental suffering. We admire, in the name of truthfulness, an art that exhibits the maximum amount of trauma, violence, physical indignity. (The question is: Do we feel it?) For us, the significant moment is the one that disturbs us most.[20]

For all its presiding authorial voice and essayistic digressions, *The Volcano Lover* also shows Sontag's new-found ability to inhabit a variety of narrative tones and moods simultaneously, both major and minor in key. The structure of the book, as Sontag pointed out in her *Paris Review* interview, was musical, borrowed from Paul Hindemith's *The Four Temperaments* (1940), beginning with three short pieces as prologue followed by four movements: 'melancholic, sanguinic, phlegmatic, choleric', of which the first two parts, almost opposites in temper, dominate *The Volcano Lover*, forming more than three-quarters of the whole.[21]

Part One, melancholic, follows the Cavaliere and his first, ideal if slightly passionless, marriage to Catherine: it is stately, brooding, thoughtful, slow. In Part Two, the centre of the novel, also told in the third person, the much more vivacious Emma enters and enlivens the narrative, which becomes literally 'sanguinic' with the spilled blood of the Revolution in Naples. Part Three, phlegmatic, is the deathbed monologue of the Cavaliere, written in the first person; while Part Four, choleric, offers other monologues from four angry women: Catherine; Emma's mother; Emma herself; and finally, the Portuguese poet Eleonora de Fonseca Pimentel.

Eleonora muses, at the close of the novel, on the fate of women in her time:

I had to forget that I was a woman to accomplish the best of which I was capable. Or I would lie to myself about how complicated it is to be a woman. Thus do all women, including the author of this book.[22]

And memorably, Eleonora, violently acerbic, gives the final assessment of all the characters in *The Volcano Lover*. Who was William Hamilton but 'an upper-class dilettante'? Who was his wife Emma 'but another talented, overwrought woman who thought herself valuable because men she could admire loved her'? As for Nelson, 'I will not deign to speak of my hatred and contempt for the warrior . . . who killed my friends.' In the novel's final lines, Eleonora gives a final, splenetic curse: 'They thought they were civilized. They were despicable. Damn them all' – a deeply unsettling, destabilizing shift of point of view.[23]

On its release in summer 1992, *The Volcano Lover* was Sontag's first ever popular success, entering the best-seller lists and being received rapturously – if with surprise that Sontag had turned her hand to what the book's subtitle called 'A Romance' – by critics. Personally, it also marked a creative high-point for Sontag, above all for the sheer gain in expressiveness she felt she had accessed in the intense three-year immersion in writing the book. She had finally proved to herself, and to the sceptical critics who had mauled her first two novels in the 1960s, that she had what it took to be a novelist. It is hard to overestimate how much this meant to Sontag; in a sense, for her, it was the most important success she ever had – one she was entirely comfortable with, as she never was with the runaway celebrity, say, of 'Notes on "Camp"'. In interviews after the appearance of the novel, she often remarked on how *The Volcano Lover* saw her finally becoming the kind of writer she always wanted to be; in her piece 'Singleness', so swept up in her creative elation of the early 1990s that she casually dismissed a lifetime's prior work, Sontag wrote that she had at last 'got to that point – it took almost thirty years – that I was finally able to write a book I really like: *The Volcano Lover*'.[24]

In January 1993, Sontag turned 60. To mark the occasion she went on a boat trip down the Nile with Leibovitz and Howard Hodgkin, about whose work she would publish one of her few essays on painting, 'About Hodgkin', which first appeared as a catalogue essay to an exhibition in 1995. Sontag respected Hodgkin's 'canny diffidence' in offering explanations of his sumptuous, slow pictures; his 'cunning design and thick, luscious colour'; his balance between figuration and abstraction; the contained emotionality of his paintings – 'The idea is to put as much as possible, of colour, of feeling, in each picture. It's as if the pictures need their broad border to contain so much feeling' – and Hodgkin's lifelong love of travel, which they both shared and were able to indulge together in Egypt.[25] (They were also in Venice together in 1994.)

> You stand at the railing of the boat going up the Nile, a day's journey from Luxor, and it's sunset. You're just looking. There are no words you are impelled to write down; you don't make a sketch or take a photograph. You look, and sometimes your eyes feel tired, and you look again, and you feel saturated, and happy, and terribly anxious.[26]

A few months after her well-earned, painterly, touristic Egypt trip, still bathing in the afterglow of *The Volcano Lover*, Sontag paid a visit to a more surprising destination for someone of her age. She flew to Sarajevo, which by April 1993 had been under Serb gunfire for a year. The initial impetus for the trip was provided by David Rieff, who was writing a book on Bosnia. Sontag stayed for only two weeks. But in that short time, during which she became friends with many people, she was incensed by the situation in the battered, besieged city. Sniper fire made everyday life in Sarajevo – even crossing the street – a game of death. 'People are killed in the place where you were just an hour before or later', Sontag wrote.[27] She became friendly with the editors of the newspaper *Oslobodenje*, which miraculously carried on publishing throughout the siege, continuing to function, unlike so many public services, such as water and electricity. Over dinner in his apartment, Kemal Kurspahic, editor-in-chief of the paper, showed Sontag bullet holes from sniper rifles in his living room.

Sontag determined to return to Sarajevo for longer, not just as a witness but 'to pitch in and do something'.[28] On her first visit, during meetings with people involved in theatre, she asked if they would like her to return and work with them. On being asked what play she would direct in Sarajevo, Sontag instantly decided on *Waiting for Godot*. The play, she thought, 'written over forty years ago, seems written for, and about, Sarajevo'.[29] When Sontag returned in July for a longer stay – over the next three years she went to Sarajevo several times each year, sometimes staying for months – she auditioned actors and began work on the production. She stayed in the Holiday Inn, which was full of war correspondents from the international dailies and weeklies. Thus, by accident, the production of *Godot* began to generate press, some of it extremely hostile and sceptical, implying that Sontag was using the play as a publicity vehicle for herself.

Like her *Trip to Hanoi* in the 1960s, though more literally so, the production of *Godot* in Sarajevo became a 'piece of political theatre'.[30] Through its wide dissemination it became a piece of performance art, a mediated statement, as much as a play. It was audacious, perhaps foolhardy, yet also an astonishing act of commitment and self-sacrifice, with quite a price of physical hardship for a 60-year-old ex-cancer-sufferer under no obligation to get involved in a European war zone, who stood to make no financial gain from the production. Sontag genuinely put her life on the line out of a sense of artistic morality, although she estimated that her chances of survival were not bad. Perhaps her willingness and bravado in this respect came from the dicing with death she had endured since her cancer, so much more likely to kill her, statistically, than sniper fire in Sarajevo. 'Some 350,000 people live in Sarajevo', Sontag said. 'Ten or 15 people die every day and around 20 get wounded. I have a one in a thousand chance.'[31] But she was still far from exempt from harm.

Waiting for Godot, under Sontag's direction in Sarajevo, merged thematically with her other work. To the consternation of Beckett purists, Sontag made the play her own, connecting it with her long-standing concern with language, communication and the theme of the couple, found especially strongly in her first two films and her 'Notes on Marriage'. Sontag had directed *As You Desire Me* in Italian, and her Swedish films were also marked by their linguistic and cultural translation, which became an integral part of their subject. For the Sarajevo *Godot*, Sontag made photocopies of the play in English, and copied in the 'Bosnian' translation line by line. She learned the foreign translation of the play which the actors spoke by heart, in ten days.[32] More radically, she divided the two parts of Vladimir and Estragon into three pairs, using six actors: a man and a woman; two women, and two men – 'three variations on the theme of the couple'.[33] The central pair of two men was 'the classic buddy pair'; the two women 'another kind of couple in which affection and dependence are mixed with exasperation and resentment: mother in her early forties and grown daughter'; and the man and woman were a quarrelsome husband and wife, modelled on the behaviour of homeless people Sontag had seen in New York.[34]

There were constant hurdles to overcome in the production. The cast had to rehearse in the dark, using only three or four candles (candles were scarce in Sarajevo, as were paperclips to bind the scripts) and hence could barely see each other, let alone their lines. They were fatigued from months of living under siege, and were also distracted by the sound of shells exploding around the city. Props – Lucky's suitcase and picnic basket; Pozzo's cigarette holder, whip and rope; even Estragon's carrot – were hard to source, as were costumes. Sontag decided to perform only the first act of *Godot*, cutting the whole of Act II, partly because of the conditions in the theatre, whose facade, lobby and cloakroom were still full of debris having been shelled a year earlier, and which had no bathroom or water for the audience, who would be hot, as it was high summer. In cutting the play in this way, Sontag also hoped to lessen its despair, feeling that the non-arrival of Godot might be hard to bear twice over in Sarajevo. Despite all the setbacks, the play opened in August to a packed theatre (tickets were free); and by the third performance on the second day of opening, Sontag felt that with the actors the play was already in good hands.

Over the next two years, Sontag continued to go back and forth to Sarajevo. By the summer of 1995 she was no longer able to come in and out by plane via Zagreb, instead having to take a perilous route by road using a trail over Mount Igman; although by November, UN planes were once again landing in the city. She remained faithful to her commitment to Sarajevo until the ceasefire and the promise of an end to the war. Yet the trips in and out of a war zone were personally distancing, bringing a certain unreality with each return to New York. It helped that Leibovitz also went to Sarajevo in July 1993, taking some superb photographs, and hence knew first-hand what it was like. Many of Susan's other friends, however, could not know, making her realize the frustrating truth of such experiences, 'that you can never really explain to them – neither how terrible it is "there" nor how bad you feel being back, "here"'.[35]

There were other journeys during these years. These were travels not into suffering and war but in pursuit of beauty. Sontag had the idea for Leibovitz's next collection of photographs to be a 'beauty book', which, Leibovitz writes, 'was to a certain extent an excuse for Susan and me to take trips'.[36] In 1994 on assignment for *Condé Nast Traveler*, Leibovitz (and Sontag) went to Jordan, a place Susan had always wanted to visit, to see the archaeological ruins at Petra. In Wadi Musa they slept in a cave with a campfire by the Monastery; a few days later they went flying in a hot-air balloon over the desert. Susan was elated, as happy as she had ever been and, after Leibovitz got out, went for a further, solo flight. The following year she also renewed her fascination with Japan, visiting the country once again and going to Kyoto.

Leibovitz was looking for a country place to buy in upstate New York. She eventually found a 200-acre estate in Rhinebeck, near the Hudson, with a barn complex in a state of disrepair. She bought the Rhinebeck property in 1996. While work on the barns was carried out, Sontag and Leibovitz moved into the old pond house on the estate; later, the pond house became the place where Susan worked, especially while writing her next novel. This was another extensive foray into the world of the past, based on the life of the actress Helena Modrzejewska, stage name Helena Modjeska, which became – after a long struggle throughout the 1990s – *In America*. Work on the book had already begun by 1993 but it took several years to take off, Susan feeling daunted by the success of *The Volcano Lover*, aware of the level of commitment she would need to summon, once again, in order to match it.

Revisiting the genre of the historical novel, Sontag was even freer with its conventions this time, yet she undertook deep research and drew heavily from sources. *In America* was 'inspired by' its real-life counterparts, Sontag wrote, 'no less and no more'. 'Most of the characters in the novel are invented, and those that are not depart in radical ways from their real-life models.'[37] In the virtuoso prelude to the novel, 'Zero', Sontag puts us in the position of the writer choosing her subject, as she tells of gatecrashing a party in a room in Krakow, which, it slowly emerges, is a reception after a play, taking place in December 1875. Eavesdropping, watching, listening, 'an alien presence',[38] the contemporary author – clearly Sontag, indulging in some autobiographical touches, mentioning her marriage to Philip Rieff, her time in Sarajevo, her childhood in Los Angeles, her ability to cope in constrained situations – sees her characters, but does not yet know who they are, what they do, or how they relate to each other. She cannot quite hear what they are saying, nor does she even understand their language. Yet she feels drawn to, entranced by, these blurrily glimpsed figures, brave enough to embark on a journey with them. She also feels the vertigo of history.

> There are so many stories to tell, it's hard to say why it's one rather than another, it must be because with this story you feel you can tell many stories, that there will be a necessity in it . . . It has to be something like falling in love.[39]

Like *The Volcano Lover*, *In America* is another story of foreigners. It is also another love triangle. But the focus this time falls much more squarely on the female lead, with whom Sontag clearly identified. *In America* follows Helena – called Maryna Zalezowska in the novel – from the height of her success in the Polish theatre to her emigration to Anaheim, California, in 1876, with her husband Count Karol Chapowski (Bogdan in the novel); her son; a young writer who is besotted with her (Ryszard); and various friends. The group start a Fourier-inspired rural commune, in search of an 'unencumbered freedom' that could hardly be theirs in Poland.[40] They strive to make their paradise work but when the commune fails, Maryna returns to the theatre, reinventing herself and touring America under the stage name Marina Zalenska. She is a triumphant success, eventually performing alongside the actor Edwin Booth.

There were several obvious elements to this story which drew Sontag in; other parts of its allure were more buried, yet chimed deeply with her concerns and her past. She was attracted to the idea of writing a novel about an actress, extending the theatrical elements of Emma Hamilton in *The Volcano Lover* much further to explore the life of a professional on the nineteenth-century stage. In 'Zero', Sontag confessed she had initially tried to write a novel set in Sarajevo (*In America* carries the dedication 'To my friends in

Sarajevo'). Although she abandoned this, in depicting her new characters she drew on her recent experiences as a theatre director in Eastern Europe. More profoundly, *In America* delves into Sontag's family roots, with its initial setting in Poland, the country of her grandparents, a country she had visited only briefly. In its portrayal of California, the novel also touches on Sontag's childhood. As she later wrote, when her Polish immigrants reached Anaheim and strolled out into the emptiness of the desert, 'I was drawing on my own memory of childhood walks into the desert of southern Arizona.'[41] And not only memory – in researching *In America*, Sontag also travelled back to California in person, in pursuit of where her characters had been: a physical journey back into her own, for so long spurned, youth.

In America, once again, sees Sontag fusing essayistic and narrative modes, planting aphorisms and digressions throughout her story. The prose is deliberately breathless, passionate, seductive, changing frequently in form, often posing as life writing, as Sontag narrates letters which give an approximation of interior monologue, or quotes from characters' diaries. The switches in focus are swift, accessing a range of varying moods and temperaments, in writing of pliant expressiveness. Sontag writes at the service of her characters, summoning all her artistic (and theatrical) energies. Part of her had always acted, or wanted to act. More and more as she got older, she saw her own early success with her essays as a form of acting – and seeing them as such is a good way to understand their sheer variety. Now she was acting in fiction. And her Polish characters on their American adventure 'seemed – and I pledged myself to be like them, on their behalf – indefatigable'.[42]

The theme of beginning again, so intrinsic to emigration, permeates the novel. With *In America* Sontag saw herself, in her sixties, continuing to begin again as a novelist; all her characters are also beginning again. In a letter from America, Maryna disavows fatalism, the Polish historical gloom that denies the possibility of change and self-transformation, the belief 'that we are all prisoners of whatever we have become'.[43] In America, Maryna does change her life, and once she takes again to the stage in her adopted country it feels 'like an escapade; like leaving home ... She was beginning again; she was rejoining her destiny; which conferred on her the rich sensation, that she had never gone astray.'[44] This was how Sontag also felt, or wanted to feel, while writing *In America*. The theme of rebeginnings reconnects with tendencies in her writing from her earliest diaries onwards, in which, even as a teenager in Tucson and Los Angeles, she pledged herself to eternal striving and reinvention as a writer. She always used writing as a way of overcoming her weaknesses, seizing her destiny, attaining a more profound, ideal self-consciousness. 'I write partly in order to change myself', Sontag said.[45] Writing must 'remind us that we can change', she vowed in a late essay.[46]

The reinvention of *In America* is tough, however. Even at the opening, Maryna is no longer young; she is tired and also ill; the emigration is difficult and beset with obstacles. Fully half of the novel traces the attempt to set up the community in Anaheim, which fails. And it is this failure that sets Maryna back towards the stage, where she has to start over from scratch, auditioning to a sceptical manager of the California Theater. In beginning again there is nothing to fall back on; one turns one's back on the past. The energy, will and nerve required to do so are formidable. Reinvention offers liberation, but has a high price. Sontag, in her personal life as much as her writing life, had learned what it means to start again from nothing. Even in Maryna's triumph there is something hard, and melancholy. Sontag practised the art of beginning again throughout her life, picking herself up, over and again, until it was a habit. She turned her weakness into strength, repeatedly, until her strength became almost a weakness.

Writing *In America* had been a struggle. By 1998, sequestered in Bari, Italy – where Sontag had gone to work on the novel and the home town of her young friend and translator Paolo Dilonardo – she finally saw her way through it. As she later told her son, she realized how she would finish it. 'Nothing can stop me now', she remembered thinking to herself.[47] A few days later, in Bari, she started to feel continually bloated, and she began to urinate blood. She knew straight away that she was ill again, and she knew it was probably cancer. But she remained in Bari to finish the book, before returning to New York. In July that year, back in America, she went for some tests, which revealed a uterine sarcoma.

At 65, suffering her second cancer, she was hurtled back into the world of chemotherapy, hospitals and agonized talks with other patients. Her illness was documented by Leibovitz, who took some time off work to be with Sontag every day as she underwent her treatment at Mount Sinai Hospital. The sense of dependence and fear that Sontag must have felt is clear from some of the photographs of her around this time, taken by her lover. She felt mentally blurry, exhausted, from the chemo, which also left her with nerve damage that made it hard to walk – and she would remain this way long afterwards. But she survived this second cancer.

In America has nine chapters. Sontag had written the first eight before her cancer – and these chapters had been rewritten and reread many times.[48] During and after her treatment she was unable to work; and concerning her nearly completed novel, she felt 'despair and fear that now I'd never finish it'.[49] But she did recover enough to do so, as the century drew to a close. Her hair had been closely cropped, and she was again living under the shadow of illness, but she resumed her hectic schedule as soon as she was able. The virtuosic final chapter of *In America*, a drunken, limping, warped dramatic monologue from the 'crushed tragedian'[50] Edwin Booth, delivered to Maryna after their performance of Shakespeare's *The Merchant of Venice*, gives Sontag's novel a conclusion that leans back to her late modernist tendencies, soaking the whole striving narrative in doubt. 'The last act has to be an anticlimax, don't you think', says Booth to Maryna, marinated in antic paradox and self-shielding, thespian layers of identity. 'As in life. Getting old is an anticlimax. Dying is, if one is lucky, an anticlimax. Who would fault a play for not ending on its highest note?'[51] As tough and unshaken as her heroine, Sontag concluded *In America* with this deft, unexpected, deliberately deflating narrative flourish, and was working furiously on the proofs of the novel at the end of 1999.

8

The Pain of Others, 2000–2004

She did not slow down. The second experience of illness –
the second taste of fear, of death – had a dual effect, bringing
melancholy moments while making Sontag appreciate life all the
more when she recovered. The sense of time expiring only made
her lust for experience greater. She spoke constantly of wanting
to continue to devote herself to work, and especially to fiction.
She already knew where her next novel would be set: in Japan.[1]
Her long-contemplated, unwritten Japan project of the 1980s
meant that she had already explored some of the territory; she
had also travelled there several times in the previous years. The
book would be a further voyage into foreignness, like *The Volcano
Lover* and *In America*. Perhaps it would also have gone some way
to completing the circle of Sontag's obsessive, inconclusive fascination, ever since her childhood, with the East. But after finishing
In America, in the familiar pattern of her writing life, Sontag was
unable not to involve herself again in other assignments – above
all, essays. She was remarkably productive as a critic in the early
years of the new century. And she continued to be a political
writer, engaged and responding to the cataclysms of world events.

Late in 1999, Leibovitz had a show, 'Women', at the Corcoran
Gallery in Washington, DC, for which Sontag wrote a catalogue
essay, 'A Photograph Is Not An Opinion. Or Is It?' The following
year, Leibovitz decided to look for an apartment to buy in Paris
– the city Susan had always spent so much time in, and where

she never really had a place of her own. One day, Leibovitz and Sontag looked at a charming, dilapidated flat right on the quai des Grands-Augustins, with tall, narrow windows giving out on to the Seine. It was hard for Sontag to climb the two flights of stairs to reach the apartment given the nerve damage in her feet from her second cancer treatment, but both Leibovitz and Sontag fell in love with the place, a former printing shop built in 1640, straight away. It was just high enough to catch the sun. 'We went back the next day and told the owner we wanted it', Leibovitz writes.[2] Picasso, they discovered, had painted *Guernica* in the same block.

In 2000 and 2001, as ever, Sontag gave talks and lectures, travelled, read and wrote. She was still discovering foreign writers, in particular, that continued to widen the international scope of her interests. She was compiling a new book of essays, *Where the Stress Falls*, published in the autumn of 2001, collecting pieces written since *Under the Sign of Saturn* in the early 1980s. This new collection is the most kaleidoscopic and mixed of all Sontag's books of essays, containing 41 relatively short pieces divided into three sections: 'Reading', 'Seeing', 'There and Here'. *Where the Stress Falls*, in some ways a mirror to *Against Interpretation* in its heterogeneity and variety, does not attempt to make the miscellaneous individual pieces advance a mission statement. But Sontag's general critical stance at this point in her life, throughout many of the pieces, was now to unashamedly defend 'high' culture from the barbarians at the gates. 'At the end of the century . . . literature, too, is besieged', she writes in her essay on Danilo Kiš, and a similar lament courses throughout the collection.[3] She had come full circle since *Against Interpretation*, with its levelling of high and low culture. Yet there was logic in her reversal – and her reversals were always honest, a recurrent feature of a mind always arguing with itself. Where in the 1960s she had been counteracting the staid hierarchies of the New York Intellectuals, by the 1990s the cultural atmosphere was anything but in need of further loosening, Sontag felt. High culture in particular was under threat, undervalued.

In *Where the Stress Falls*, Sontag remains a tirelessly informed admirer of a range of work in different media. In a reappraisal of *Against Interpretation*, 'Thirty Years Later', included in the new book, Sontag recalls her arrival in New York in the 1960s, determined to be true to 'my idea of a writer – someone interested in "everything"'.[4] The new collection reveals that she had stayed true to that ideal. Of all Sontag's books of essays, *Where the Stress Falls* most conveys her roving avidity, moving across literature, cinema, painting, dance, opera, photography, politics and travel. If the collection does not advance any particular critical or cultural theory, it does have a common theme in travel – and its epigraph, and the title of one of its pieces, comes from Elizabeth Bishop's poem 'Questions of Travel'.

Sontag had shaken off the commanding, anti-autobiographical, self-consciously overreaching stance of her earlier essays. She now writes in a looser, more intimate way, sometimes using fragments of reflection from her own life. These later essays were no longer highly-strung tapestries of aphorism and assertion, and to earlier admirers can seem disconcertingly keen to state the obvious. But Sontag wanted to break the voice, and the way she wrote, in her earlier essays, when she hit a block with them in the 1980s; and the warmth and candour in *Where the Stress Falls* are entirely new. After more than four decades as a professional writer, she writes from much closer to herself. She is more playful in the styles of her criticism, as in the pieces on dance, which often recall Gertrude Stein.

She also writes more about the art of fiction in *Where the Stress Falls* than ever before. The opening section, on 'Reading', is her most extensive collection of pieces on fiction yet, and many parts of 'There and Here' reflect on the process of writing. Although Sontag is now more traditional than in her earliest criticism, which pursued the new, she still defends a distinctively experimental, global line of fiction, where the ludic risks of Borges, Cervantes and Sterne hold sway. Sontag's appreciation of American and British literature remains deliberately limited. The title essay in the collection, the only piece about U.S. fiction, connects novels by Glenway Wescott (*The Pilgrim Hawk*, 1940), Randall Jarrell (*Pictures from an Institution*, 1954) and Elizabeth Hardwick (*Sleepless Nights*, 1979). Even the American writers Sontag repeatedly said she admired – Donald Barthelme, Joan Didion, William Gass, Leonard Michaels and Grace Paley – did not become the subjects of essays by her. Instead, the literary pieces in *Where the Stress Falls* range across the world, especially Eastern Europe, taking in Boris Pasternak, Osip Mandelstam and Marina Tsvetaeva (Russia); Machado de Assis (Brazil); W. G. Sebald (Germany, England); Adam Zagajewski (Poland); Robert Walser (Germany); Danilo Kiš (Hungary, Yugoslavia); Witold Gombrowicz (Poland); and Juan Rulfo (Mexico).

Reading had been a form of travelling for Sontag from her earliest youth; it remained so right into her last years. In 'There and Here' Sontag writes, in a piece on her love for the travel writer Richard Halliburton: 'before there was travel – in my life, at least – there were travel books. Books that told you the world was very large but quite encompassable. Full of destinations.'[5] Her reading was a catalogue of such destinations: books and places merged. Hence the love of foreign literature, and the scorn for chroniclers of American reality such as Philip Roth or John Updike. Travel, more and more, had become a vital thread in Sontag's life, as the pieces gathered in 'There and Here' show; gradually she had learned to fuse her aesthetic delight in new places with her moral concerns. Visiting new countries, reading work from other places, became for Sontag part of the responsibility of being a writer.

The same boundless curiosity and internationality also marks the section of *Where the Stress Falls* on 'Seeing'. Sontag's taste in films, especially during her most keen cinema-going period in the 1960s and '70s, had also been related to travel and to understanding other countries, other worlds. Now, as she writes in her essay 'A Century of Cinema' (1995), in an elegiac mode best seen as explaining her own abandonment of cinema as a subject for criticism since the 1980s, the cinephilia that marked her youth was on the wane, and cinema itself – 'once heralded as *the* art of the twentieth century' – seemingly dying.[6] Apart from a piece on Rainer Werner Fassbinder, this is the only piece on film in the collection, so unlike Sontag's earlier books of essays, which always contained major film studies. The visual senses are appeased, instead, by a diverse sheaf of appreciative pieces: on Bunraku theatre; garden history; Dutch painting; Howard Hodgkin; dance; Wagner; Italian photography; E. J. Bellocq; Polly Borland; Robert Mapplethorpe; Annie Leibovitz's 'Women'. Part of the reason for this eclecticism lay in the long gestation of the collection, gathering loose prefaces, catalogue essays and reviews from nearly two decades.

Some of the last pieces in *Where the Stress Falls* appeared in various periodicals during 2000 and 2001. Sontag was also working up other essays in these months, eventually collected in *At the Same Time*, a final essay-volume published in 2007. Among these were essays on the letters between Tsvetaeva, Pasternak and Rilke; and a wonderful piece on the Russian writer Leonid Tsypkin, author of *Summer in Baden-Baden*, for which Sontag engaged in some detailed research, corresponding with Tsypkin's family, and in which she related how, almost as in the opening of *The Volcano Lover*, she had come across Tsypkin's work one day while 'rifling through a bin of scruffy-looking used paperbacks' outside a second-hand bookstore on London's Charing Cross Road.[7]

Around this time, now just into her fifties, Leibovitz became pregnant. She had wanted a baby for years, and by September 2001 was nearly due to give birth. For ten days early in the month, Sontag was in Berlin. She had planned to spend all of 11 September writing, in a suburb of the city. Phone calls from Bari and New York alerted her to the terrorist attacks on the World Trade Center in Manhattan, in close view from where she and Leibovitz lived. Leibovitz was at her doctor's that morning, having the heartbeat of her baby monitored. In Berlin, Sontag spent the next 48 hours watching the attacks and their aftermath on CNN.[8]

Her indignation and distance from what was happening, so close to her own home in America, resulted in an indignant piece for the *New Yorker* about the rhetoric of the media coverage of the event, roundly castigating Americans for their response to the attacks. 'The disconnect between what happened and how it might be understood, and the self-righteous drivel and outright deceptions being peddled by virtually all our public figures . . . is startling, depressing. The voices licensed to follow the event seem to have joined together in a campaign to infantilize the public', Sontag wrote.[9] She objected to the grandly ahistorical, psychotherapeutic coverage of the disaster, the lack of awareness of past American foreign policy, the proclamations of American strength and threats of retaliation, the absence of mature democratic debate. Of course, her piece provoked a strong reaction, an outcry. It was not the best time to be acting as a scourge on the nation's conscience, and Sontag's latent anti-American leanings, for all her inescapable Americanness, simmered beneath her angry words. She had never been able to reconcile herself to America, or even to American culture. As a critic, a novelist, a film-maker and a playwright, she had so often avoided the subject of contemporary America – but many of her political and polemical pieces tackled her home country directly.

In a piece a few weeks later for the Italian newspaper *il manifesto*, Sontag was more reflective, sympathetic, almost contrite. After she dashed off her 9/11 'diatribe', she wrote: 'real grief followed in not altogether coherent stages, as it always does when one is removed from, and therefore deprived of full contact with, the reality of loss.'[10] (She could here have been referring, as she often did even in these late years, to the unreality of the loss of her father. She had recently hired a researcher, in 1998, to find Jack Rosenblatt's grave.[11]) 'Returning to New York late at night the following week,' Sontag wrote:

> I drove directly from Kennedy Airport to as close as I could get by car to the site of the attack, and spent an hour prowling on foot around what is now a steaming, mountainous, foul-smelling mass graveyard – some six hectares large – in the southern part of Manhattan. In those first days after my return to New York, the reality of the devastation, and the immensity of the loss of life, made my initial focus on the rhetoric surrounding the event seem to me less relevant.[12]

Sontag also went on a tour of Ground Zero with Leibovitz. She had noted, in her *New Yorker* piece, the 'disconnect' between what had happened and how it was mediated; she could also hardly help but feel the disconnect between how she had viewed the event in Berlin and her emotions as she stood in the ruins. All these conflicting thoughts informed her conception of *Regarding the Pain of Others* which, as with so many of her books, arose partly out of self-correction. But for a few months, at least, at the close of the year, Sontag's focus turned, joyfully, to new life, for on 16 October 2001, Annie Leibovitz gave birth to Sarah Cameron Leibovitz, at the Roosevelt Hospital in New York. Susan was by her side during the birth, holding the freshly delivered Sarah in her hands as she arrived and was wrapped in a blanket. It had been nearly 50 years since Susan had given birth at nineteen to David, in September 1952; once again, nearer the end than the beginning of her life this time, she was holding a newborn baby.

Sontag wrote fewer occasional pieces the following year, when she worked mainly on *Regarding the Pain of Others*, her last book.

She gathered folders of research notes and clippings for the project, gathered under various headings: 'War and Photography', 'War 2003', 'Apathy and Cruelty'.[13] The book was written as the American 'war on terror' following 9/11 gathered pace with the invasion of Afghanistan and Iraq. In its opening pages, Sontag referred at length to another book composed during the onset of global conflict, Virginia Woolf's *Three Guineas*, 'her brave, unwelcomed reflections on the roots of war', published, as Sontag noted, in June 1938.[14]

Regarding the Pain of Others, another book-length extended essay, is a follow-up to *On Photography*, taking as its subject the dilemmas posed by contemplating images of suffering, death and war. In this, it returns to Sontag's core theme, the interplay of ethics and aesthetics. It is also another exploration of surrealist radical juxtaposition, looking at the disjunctions created by mediated reportage. As ever, Sontag drew from her relationships: the twin subjects, war and photography, were closely associated with Leibovitz's work as a photographer, and David's writing as a war correspondent. Much of the tension of the essay lies outside its pages, in the links between its arguments, ranging across history, and the exigencies of the particular historical moment in which it was written. What might merely have been an art historical or ethical study gains an irrefutable urgency from its commentary on matters that, in the early years of the twenty-first century, were affecting American citizens daily, as battles being fought on their behalf filled newspapers and TV channels, just as they did decades before while Sontag was writing *Death Kit*.

'Being a spectator of calamities taking place in another country is a quintessential modern experience', Sontag writes.[15] *Regarding the Pain of Others* shows that, modern as it is, this is also a conundrum with a long history. The thirst we have for images of pain is deeply rooted. As in *On Photography*, Sontag fills in, very subtly, the history of war reportage and its changing authenticity, censorship and use of different media. The Crimean War, the American Civil War, indeed every war until the First World War, took place largely 'beyond the camera's ken', even as they had their great photographers such as Roger Fenton and Mathew Brady.[16] Even the images of the First World War were generally of an aftermath rather than the action itself. The first conflict 'covered' by war photographers, Sontag writes, was the Spanish Civil War – 'it was precisely in the late 1930s that the profession of bearing individual witness to war and war's atrocities with a camera was forged' – while Vietnam was 'the first to be witnessed day after day by television cameras'. Larry Burrows, in Vietnam working for *Life*, 'was the first important photographer to do a whole war in color'.[17]

Sontag also ranges further back into the iconography of suffering, discussing various etchings from the sixteenth to the nineteenth centuries by Hendrik Goltzius (*Dragon Devouring the Companions of Cadmus*, 1588), Jacques Callot (*The Miseries and Misfortunes of War*, 1633) and Francisco Goya (*The Disasters of War*, 1863). For Sontag, Goya's sequence of 83 etchings, an atrocity exhibition meant 'to awaken, shock, wound', 'an assault on the sensibility of the viewer', marks 'a turning point in the history of moral feelings', demanding new levels of responsiveness, shaking the viewer into awareness.[18]

In *Regarding the Pain of Others*, one of Sontag's deep subjects is, again, attention. Through the lens of discussing war photography, Sontag trains the reader's mind on war, on the power – or otherwise – of art to arouse the imagination, the viewer's sympathy, focusing especially on the distortions and failings of sympathy imposed by the structures of photographic and televisual 'news'. She drew heavily on her experience of being in war-torn Sarajevo and her subsequent returns to New York, which taught her that for all the mediation of the Sarajevan sniper attacks, which reached American living rooms night after night via CNN, the conflict remained stubbornly remote in American minds. People simply

Francisco Goya, 'Even Worse', plate 22 of *The Disasters of War* (1810, pub. 1863).

did not care or understand. In a more unstated way, Sontag also drew on her recent feelings during 9/11 and the news coverage of Afghanistan and Iraq, which showed her the importance of being present at the site of suffering. She lambasts theories of 'the death of reality' – the idea that reality itself had dissolved, existing only through media – as 'a breathtaking provincialism' that denies the realities of suffering in many parts of the world, always so much larger than the mediated diffusion of it.[19] She wonders whether others' pain might be conveyed more deeply by narratives rather than images, by photographs rather than television. She had been vigorously against television since the 1960s. In this, she sometimes seemed reactionary or stubborn. Yet Sontag was one of the first writers to acknowledge the impact of television and of heavy doses of mediation on feeling, on irony – she was always unfashionably serious, never lightly ironic – and on understanding: themes central to a younger generation of American writers, most notably David Foster Wallace.

No mediation, no representation, can make us feel the full pain of others. But there is a moral obligation, Sontag writes, to acknowledge suffering, and thus to contemplate existing records of it. It is a moral education, in itself a painful one, to understand how much suffering there is in the world and to gauge the extent of human indifference and human depravity. 'No one after a certain age has the right to this kind of innocence, of superficiality, to this degree of ignorance, or amnesia', she avers. Sontag counters her assertion in *On Photography* that saturation in such images might have a diminishing effect, making us care less than ever. But she ends her long meditation on suffering by coming down finally against art's ability to convey such realities. 'We don't get it. We truly can't imagine what it was like. We can't imagine how dreadful, how terrifying war is; and how normal it becomes', Sontag writes in conclusion. 'That's what every soldier, and every journalist and aid worker and independent observer who has put in time under fire . . . stubbornly feels. And they are right.'[20]

Regarding the Pain of Others was published early in 2003, and Sontag celebrated her 70th birthday in January that year. She holidayed with Annie and Sarah, now one year old, in the Bahamas over the winter, at Harbor Island. Throughout 2003, Sontag continued to work at several essays – alongside her novel set in Japan, she had now promised herself another book collection of criticism, 'my last one'.[21] Early in 2004 she continued the work of *Regarding the Pain of Others* with her last major published essay, 'Regarding the Torture of Others', about the photographs from Abu Ghraib, which reflected on the present, destabilized, newly democratic yet disturbing coordinates of war photography in the twenty-first century.

Where once photographing war was the province of photo-journalists, now the soldiers themselves are all photographers – recording their war, their fun, their observations of what they find picturesque, their atrocities – and swapping images among themselves, and e-mailing them around the globe.

'The photographs *are* us', Sontag writes unsparingly, indicting not only the people who took them but American culture generally.[22]

Ever aware of new technologies, Sontag puts her finger on the new century's aesthetic – 'more and more recording of what people do, by themselves'[23] – while also relating it back to Andy Warhol, who filmed her *Screen Test* all those years ago. Towards the end of her life she was thinking more and more about the effects, for art and above all for the novel, of the new, digital age of endless recording and dissemination. Sontag had always been an oppositional writer, ever since *Against Interpretation*. Now it was not interpretation that was the main danger for her, but information. In March 2004 in South Africa she delivered a lecture defending the novel against hypertext and television, in particular in the novel's artful sense of completion, of ending, as opposed to the untrammelled flow of information available through television or the Internet.

'A novel is *not* a set of proposals, or a list, or a collection of agendas, or an (open-ended, revisable) itinerary. It is the journey itself – made, experienced, and completed', Sontag writes.[24] She had learned this the hard way. She was more prone to multiplicity and possibility than anyone. Her criticism and diaries, especially, *were* full of lists and sets of proposals; it had taken the best part of her life to learn how to contain the desire she felt to explore new avenues of knowledge in linear prose narrative. She always moved on, took up new positions, discovered new arts, new writers, new forms, making her criticism so fresh and entrancing for others to follow. All her work intersected, crossing from one genre to another. She denied some parts of her talent, above all her skill as a critic, but every part of her oeuvre, finally, was interlinked. Sontag could not have been the novelist she was if she was not a critic; she could not have been the critic she was if she was not a novelist. She could not have made the films she made if she had not also written about film; she could not have written the plays she wrote if she had not also directed theatre. Her novels were often like essays, her films like plays, her essays like performances. She always excelled in translating arts from one genre to another, from one country or culture to another. She stretched forms and styles. She learned from everything.

As Wayne Koestenbaum writes, Sontag

ate the world . . . gobbled up sensations, genres, concepts. She swallowed political and aesthetic movements. She devoured roles: diplomat, filmmaker, scourge, novelist, gadfly, essayist, night owl, bibliophile, cineaste . . . She tried to prove how much a human life – a writer's life – could include. Like Walter Benjamin, she was entranced by multiplicity.[25]

Yet at 71, she was thinking about endings, exclusion, conclusion, just as much as she was, by habit, still thinking about new projects. Endings, she now stated in her lecture, were almost the point of the novel, seen in opposition to to hypertext or television. Endings, the sense of borders and enclosure around a story, were crucial. Yet an ending that feels truly natural is hard for the writer to attain; 'the construction of a plot consists of finding moments of stability, and then generating new narrative tensions that undo these moments – until the ending is reached', she writes.

What we call a 'proper' ending of a novel is another equilibrium – one that, if it is properly designed, will have a recognizably different status. It will – this ending – persuade us that the tensions belonging to any difficult story have been sufficiently answered for. They have lost their power to effect further meaningful changes. They are held in check by the ending's capacity to seal everything in. Endings in a novel confer a kind of liberty that life stubbornly denies us: to come to a full stop that is not death . . .[26]

Did she know, even subconsciously, writing this, that she was dying? For several years now, Sontag had been fixated on the pain of others. The moral activism of her late work had meant that she was still constantly concerned with other people, looking outwards at the world rather than inwards at her own life and health. But she herself had also been in pain ever since her second cancer and was by this stage, writing in early 2004 – though she cannot have known to what extent – very seriously ill. As David Rieff relates, Susan had suffered several serious medical problems, including pleurisy and a collapsed lung, the previous year. Her housekeeper had noticed that she was bruising easily, in places on her body suggesting that these bruises were not from physical accidents. When questioned about this, Susan changed the subject. She did not tell David or Paolo Dilonardo, whom she would often confide in on other matters, about it.

That March, the same month that she gave the lecture in Cape Town, Susan had gone in for her regular twice-yearly scan and blood tests. One of the blood tests was ominous. David was in Jerusalem and the West Bank, researching a magazine story, for most of the month. When he returned to New York at the end of March, Susan told him she might be ill once again. He accompanied her to the doctor for the results of some of the tests. Susan was told she had MDS, or myelodysplastic syndrome, a form of blood cancer that would eventually become full-blown leukaemia. There was no chance of recovery. There was nothing that could be done. Susan stared out of the window of the car on the drive back to the apartment with David, maintaining a steady, appallingly uncomfortable, silence. Finally, she turned to him. "'Wow", she said. "Wow".'[27]

Never a fatalist, Susan refused to accept what she probably knew, at least in the early days after her diagnosis. She had always railed against defeatism, even in the matter of illness, and her will to knowledge, her submission to the best treatment and her sheer determination in the face of sickness had kept her alive through two cancers. This time, the third time, she was also determined to not be defeated. On her return from the doctor she began the now almost familiar search for information about her illness. But this time, there was no positive aspect to the information gathering. The more she found out, the more she realized how little hope there was. Yet she persisted, even strenuously believed, almost until the moment of her death, that she would recover and return to the life she so loved. She persisted in her own denial of death, so deeply rooted.

In his memoir of his mother's final illness, *Swimming in a Sea of Death*, David Rieff circles obsessively over what happened in 2004. 'In the aftermath of her visit to Dr. A', Rieff writes, 'my mother could find room for little else but despair', but 'the habits of hope survived her loss of it'. Susan picked herself up and carried on, refusing to reconcile herself to the sense of an ending, and resolution of tension, which she had recently praised as a key quality in fiction, immersing herself instead in the flow of endless possibility that had always come so naturally to her, her illusion of always re-beginning, of being at the start of something new, re-stoking the sources of her desires. She had three different book projects on the go now: a third, more autobiographical work on illness, her 'last' book of essays, and her Japan novel. Yet for all that, in the first weeks of her last illness, as she oscillated between a hyperactive intensity and a melancholic somnolence, 'she would walk around the flat as if not quite sure where she was . . . now, she acted as if it were not the kingdom of the ill she was entering but the kingdom of the dying. She knew. In those early days, *she* knew.'[28]

'To go on living: perhaps that was her way of dying', says Rieff in his memoir, brutal towards its author in its self-accusations, mainly for what he sees as his own collusion with his mother's inability to face the fact that she was dying.[29] Susan did not want to talk with David about the prospect of dying, and he was astonished at how she kept up the pretence of continuing life.

Rieff's memoir overlooks – naturally, blindly, poignantly – the possibility that Susan was also trying to spare her son from the truth, or that she was hoping they could both huddle in a shared denial of her swiftly – but also agonizingly slowly – oncoming death. She could not stand to be alone – less than ever, in the months of her illness – and the apartment was filled with a stream of friends and visitors who, as in 'The Way We Live Now', were in constant, anxious communication with each other about the state of Susan's health.

There was one hope of recovery: a bone marrow transplant. Mid-2004, Sontag was flown to Seattle for the operation. During the three months after the transplant, she suffered almost constant illness and infection. Leibovitz flew in for weekends, kept things in check, and talked to Susan. By November it was clear that the transplant had failed. Sontag went back to New York on an air ambulance, to Memorial Sloan-Kettering Cancer Center. She still spoke of what she would do when she got out of hospital. About to turn 72 in January, she still wanted to '*see* more, to *hear* more, to *feel* more', as she had put it in *Against Interpretation*,[30] though the tensions in her own life, also a 'difficult story', had largely, extraordinarily, been resolved. She had been thinking and writing about death all her life; it was an endless subject for her.

As she sat beside her mother's bedside in Hawaii as she died in December 1986, Mildred's last words to Susan were '"Why don't you go back to the hotel?" To which Susan replied, "Oh, you know, mother, I love hospitals." And her mother smiled and closed her eyes. "She liked that, you see. She thought it witty and sarcastic. I couldn't say, "I've come here because I love you. I've come because you are mortally ill".[31] The day before Susan died, on 28 December 2004, she had been talking to herself, about her mother, and Joseph Brodsky. She called out for David, who was sitting right next to her bed.

My mother did not open her eyes, or move her head. For a moment, I thought that she had fallen back to sleep. But after a pause, she said, 'I want to tell you . . .' That was all she said . . . These were the last words my mother spoke to me.[32]

References

1 Beginnings, 1933–1950

1 Susan Sontag, *As Consciousness is Harnessed to Flesh: Diaries, 1964–1980*, ed. David Rieff (London, 2012), pp. 348–9.
2 David Rieff mentions this in Susan Sontag, *Reborn: Early Diaries, 1947–1963*, ed. David Rieff (London, 2009), p. 106; and in his preface to *As Consciousness*, p. vii.
3 See, for example, Leland Poague, ed., *Conversations with Susan Sontag* (Jackson, MS, 1995), p. 228.
4 Carl Rollyson and Lisa Paddock, *Susan Sontag: The Making of an Icon* (New York, 2000), p. 4.
5 Poague, ed., *Conversations*, p. 53.
6 *Reborn*, p. 117.
7 Susan Sontag, 'Project for a Trip to China', in *I, Etcetera* (London, 2001), p. 5.
8 Ibid., pp. 5–6.
9 *Reborn*, pp. 115 (whistle), 107 (parsley), 120 ('handkerchief' and 'ring'), 108 ('wallet'), 116 ('singing'), 122 ('dreams'), 116 ('dead').
10 Ibid., p. 108.
11 'Project for a Trip to China', p. 6.
12 This plan for the China book is outlined in Sontag's diaries. See *As Consciousness*, pp. 328–34.
13 'Project for a Trip to China', pp. 11–12.
14 Ibid., p. 8.
15 *Reborn*, p. 124.
16 'Project for a Trip to China', p. 24.
17 Joan Acocella, 'The Hunger Artist', *New Yorker* (6 March 2000), p. 72.

18 'Project for a Trip to China', p. 11.

19 *As Consciousness*, p. 220.

20 Ibid., p. 220.

21 *Reborn*, p. 106.

22 Poague, ed., *Conversations*, p. 133.

23 All these memories are in 'Notes of a Childhood', in *Reborn*, pp. 121–4.

24 Susan Sontag, interview with Edward Hirsch, 'The Art of Fiction', *The Paris Review*, 137 (1995), pp. 177–209; *Reborn*, p. 109.

25 'Project for a Trip to China', p. 9.

26 *Reborn*, p. 110.

27 Susan Sontag, 'Pilgrimage', *New Yorker* (21 December 1987), p. 39.

28 Ibid., pp. 38–9.

29 'The Art of Fiction', pp. 177–209.

30 Barbara Ching notes that the title 'Pilgrimage' was chosen late in the compositional process. See Barbara Ching, '"Not Even a New Yorker": Susan Sontag in America', in *The Scandal of Susan Sontag*, ed. Barbara Ching and Jennifer A. Wagner-Lawlor (New York, 2009), p. 54; 'Pilgrimage', p. 39.

31 'Pilgrimage', p. 38.

32 Ibid., p. 38.

33 Ibid., p. 39.

34 Poague, ed., *Conversations*, p. 190.

35 'Pilgrimage', p. 42.

36 Ibid., pp. 40, 41.

37 *Reborn*, pp. 11, 20.

38 Ibid., p. 24.

39 Rollyson and Paddock, *Susan Sontag*, p. 27.

40 *Reborn*, p. 28.

41 Poague, ed., *Conversations*, p. 274.

42 *Reborn*, p. 56.

43 'Pilgrimage', p. 46.

44 *Reborn*, pp. 71, 73.

2 Notes on Marriage, 1951–1958

1 Susan Sontag, *Reborn*: *Early Diaries, 1947–1963*, ed. David Rieff (London, 2009), p. 89.

2 Ibid., pp. 43–4.

3 Susan Sontag, *As Consciousness is Harnessed to Flesh: Diaries, 1964–1980*, ed. David Rieff (London, 2012), p. 361.

4 Sontag in Phillip Lopate, *Notes on Sontag* (Princeton, NJ, 2009), p. 78.

5 Susan Sontag, 'The Letter Scene', *New Yorker* (18 August 1986), p. 28.

6 *As Consciousness*, p. 5.

7 Ibid., p. 336.

8 *Reborn*, pp. 83, 88–9.

9 Ibid., pp. 100–01.

10 Ibid., p. 119.

11 Carl Rollyson points this out in Carl Rollyson and Lisa Paddock, *Susan Sontag: The Making of an Icon* (New York, 2000), p. 41.

12 Sigrid Nunez, *Sempre Susan* (New York, 2011), p. 124.

13 Philip Toynbee, 'Critique of Freud', *Encounter* (April 1960), pp. 73–5.

14 Susan Sontag, *Illness as Metaphor and AIDS and Its Metaphors* (London, 2002), p. 3.

15 Philip Rieff, *Freud: The Mind of the Moralist* (New York, 1961), p. xx.

16 Ibid., p. 84.

17 More evidence that this passage comparing Schwitters's *Merz* constructions and psychoanalysis was written by Sontag can be found in its reappearance, with very slight differences in wording, in Sontag's essay on 'happenings'. See Susan Sontag, 'Happenings: An Art of Radical Juxtaposition', in *Against Interpretation* (London, 2001), p. 270; Rieff, *Freud*, pp. 83–4.

18 Rieff, *Freud*, pp. 338–9.

19 *Reborn*, p. 191: 'I did desire Philip tremendously during the first year.'

20 Ibid., p. 103.

21 Ibid., p. 141.

22 Ibid., p. 150.

23 'The Letter Scene', p. 27.

24 *Reborn*, pp. 147, 149.

25 'The Letter Scene', p. 28.

26 *Reborn*, p. 181.

27 Ibid., pp. 196, 191.

28 Rollyson and Paddock, *Susan Sontag*, p. 42.

29 *Reborn*, pp. 179, 186 (Pirandello), 183 (Racine), 192 (Brecht), 193 (Genet).

30 Ibid., pp. 175 (Rouch), 198 (Stroheim), 178 (Carné).

31 Rollyson and Paddock, *Susan Sontag*, p. 46.

32 Alice Kaplan, *Dreaming in French: The Paris Years of Jacqueline Bouvier Kennedy, Susan Sontag, and Angela Davis* (Chicago, IL, 2012), p. 98.

33 Harriet Sohmers Zwerling, 'A Memoir of Alfred Chester', *Raritan*, XII/3 (Winter 1993), reprinted in Harriet Sohmers Zwerling, *Notes of a Nude Model* (New York, 2003), and as an Afterword to Alfred Chester, *Jamie is My Heart's Desire* (Boston, MA, 2007), p. 269.

34 Harriet Sohmers Zwerling, 'Memories of Sontag: From an Ex-Pat's Diary' (entry for 5 February 1958), *The Brooklyn Rail* (2006).

35 *Reborn*, p. 188.

36 Sohmers Zwerling, 'Memories of Sontag' (entry for 25 February 1958).

37 *Reborn*, pp. 189, 195.

38 'The Letter Scene', p. 31.

39 *Reborn*, p. 200.

40 Sohmers Zwerling, 'Memories of Sontag' (entry for 23 June 1958).

41 Ibid.

42 *Reborn*, p. 209.

43 Susan Sontag, *In America* (London, 2001), p. 24.

44 Sontag in Nunez, *Sempre Susan*, p. 124.

45 Leland Poague, ed., *Conversations with Susan Sontag* (Jackson, MS, 1995), p. 266.

3 New York! New York! 1959–1965

1 Susan Sontag, *Reborn: Early Diaries, 1947–1963*, ed. David Rieff (London, 2009), p. 211.

2 Carl Rollyson and Lisa Paddock, *Susan Sontag: The Making of an Icon* (New York, 2000), p. 52.

3 David Rieff, *Swimming in a Sea of Death: A Son's Memoir* (London, 2008), p. 68.

4 Rollyson and Paddock, *Susan Sontag*, p. 51.

5 This quotation from the diaries is in Rieff, *Swimming*, p. 141.

6 Rollyson and Paddock, *Susan Sontag*, p. 53.

7 Ibid., p. 54.

8 *Reborn*, p. 227.

9 Ibid., p. 221.

10 Susan Sontag, *As Consciousness is Harnessed to Flesh: Diaries, 1964–1980*, ed. David Rieff (London, 2012), p. 233.

11 Edward Field, *The Man Who Would Marry Susan Sontag* (Madison, WI, 2005), p. 163.

12 Cynthia Ozick, *Foreign Bodies* (London, 2011), p. 61.

13 Edward Field, 'The Mystery of Alfred Chester', *Boston Review*, XVIII/2 (1993).

14 *Jamie is My Heart's Desire* was published in England in 1956, and in America the following year. It was also published in French in 1956 as *Deuil fantaisie* ('Fantasy Mourning').

15 Cynthia Ozick, 'Alfred Chester's Wig', *New Yorker* (30 March 1992), p. 92.

16 Diana Athill, afterword to Alfred Chester, *The Exquisite Corpse* (Boston, MA, 2003), p. 242, adapted from Diana Athill, *Stet: A Memoir* (London, 2000).

17 *Reborn*, p. 246.

18 Field, *The Man Who Would Marry Susan Sontag*, p. 108.

19 Ibid., p. 109.

20 David Rieff notes Sontag's use of Dexamyl in *As Consciousness*, p. 11.

21 Joan Acocella, 'The Hunger Artist', *New Yorker* (6 March 2000), p. 75.

22 In *Notes on Sontag*, Phillip Lopate recalls seeing Sontag sometimes on her way to the New Yorker Theater, where she claimed she had a free pass. Lopate, *Notes on Sontag* (Princeton, NJ, 2009), p. 41.

23 *Reborn*, p. 257.

24 Lopate, *Notes on Sontag*, pp. 37–8.

25 Sontag, interview in the *Paris Review*, 137 (1995), pp. 177–209; the account of writing the first lines of *The Benefactor* is in *Conversations with Susan Sontag*, ed. Leland A. Poague (Jackson, MS, 1995), p. 227.

26 In the preface, 'A Note and Some Acknowledgments', to *Against Interpretation* (London, 2001), p. vii, Sontag says that she finished *The Benefactor* in early 1962.

27 *Reborn*, p. 237.

28 Leonard Woolf wrote of Freud's 'aim to show that it is the "dark half" of the mind which in the perfectly normal waking man produces all kinds of trivial errors and slips and rememberings, and which under other conditions will, following the same laws, produce the absurd fantasies of sleep or the terrible fantasies of madness'. Woolf's review marks out the terrain of *The Benefactor*. Leonard Woolf, 'Review of Freud's *Psychopathology of Everyday Life*', *New Weekly*, 1/13 (June 1914), p. 412. Reprinted in S. P. Rosenbaum, ed., *A Bloomsbury Group Reader* (Oxford, 1993), p. 191.

29 Philip Rieff, *Freud: The Mind of the Moralist* (New York, 1961), p. 57; Susan Sontag, *The Benefactor* (London, 2009), p. 1.

30 *As Consciousness*, p. 237.

31 *The Benefactor*, p. 265.

32 Ibid., p. 41.

33 *As Consciousness*, p. 231.

34 *The Benefactor*, p. 4.

35 Ibid., p. 113.

36 Ibid., p. 63.

37 Poague, ed., *Conversations*, p. 43.

38 *The Benefactor*, p. 8.

39 Rieff, *Freud*, p. 204.

40 *As Consciousness*, p. 190.

41 *The Benefactor*, p. 97.

42 Susan Sontag, 'At the Same Time: The Novelist and Moral Reasoning', in *At the Same Time*, ed. Paolo Dilonardo and Anne Jump (London, 2007), p. 210.

43 *The Benefactor*, p. 32.

44 *Reborn*, p. 240.

45 Ibid., p. 261.

46 Field, *The Man Who Would Marry Susan Sontag*, p. 115.

47 Ibid., p. 132.

48 Rollyson and Paddock, *Susan Sontag*, pp. 78–9.

49 *Reborn*, p. 318.

50 Poague, ed., *Conversations*, p. 208.

51 'Writing Itself: On Roland Barthes' was the introduction to Susan Sontag, ed., *A Barthes Reader* (New York, 1982). It is also collected in Susan Sontag, *Where the Stress Falls* (London, 2003), pp. 63–88.

Sontag mentions the six-month gestation of the essay in Poague, ed., *Conversations*, p. 207.

52 Susan Sontag, 'Against Interpretation', in *Against Interpretation* (London, 2001), p. 13.

53 Ibid., p. 14.

54 Acocella, 'The Hunger Artist', p. 73.

55 Susan Sontag, 'Happenings: An Art of Radical Juxtaposition', in *Against Interpretation*, pp. 269–71.

56 Poague, ed., *Conversations*, p. 36; the Burroughs essay in these translations largely came from Sontag's entry 'Literature', in *Great Ideas Today, 1966*, ed. Robert M. Hutchins and Mortimer J. Adler (New York, 1966), pp. 146–91. See Leland Poague and Kathy A. Parsons, *Susan Sontag: An Annotated Bibliography, 1948–1992* (New York, 2000), pp. 151–3.

57 Susan Sontag, 'Notes on "Camp"', in *Against Interpretation*, pp. 275 ('the sensibility'), 276–7.

58 Ibid., p. 277.

59 Ibid., p. 289.

60 For reproductions and a commentary on Sontag's *Screen Tests*, the best resource is Callie Angell, *Andy Warhol Screen Tests: The Films of Andy Warhol, Catalogue Raisonné* (New York, 2006), vol. I, pp. 188–91.

61 *As Consciousness*, p. 26.

62 Ibid., pp. 56 ('weightless'), 72.

63 Ibid., pp. 61 (Rieff), 80 ('to see more').

64 Ibid., pp. 83 (at Edisto Beach), 86 (a novel).

65 Ibid., pp. 98 (letters), 97 (suicide).

66 Rieff, *Swimming*, p. 76.

67 *As Consciousness*, pp. 62–3.

68 Ibid., p. 66.

69 Sontag describes the 'Thomas Faulk' project as 'abandoned' in *As Consciousness*, p. 363.

70 Ibid., pp. 88, 363, 131.

71 See Field, *The Man Who Would Marry Susan Sontag*, p. 139. Bowles wrote to Edward Field years later about how he prepared Dris to meet Alfred. 'The first time I met that young man,' Bowles wrote to Field of Dris, 'I decided never to have anything to do with him. He struck me as bad news, and I admit I was afraid of him. His conversation

consisted solely of accounts of assaults he had made on European men, and this seemed to me a very bad sign. So (this may sound like a non sequitur) as soon as Alfred wrote me he was definitely coming to Morocco, I began to coach Dris on how to behave with him . . . I was curious to see what would happen . . .'.

72 *As Consciousness*, p. 108.
73 Ibid., pp. 120, 123.
74 Ibid., p. 111.
75 Ibid., p. 123.

4 Styles of Radical Will, 1966–1968

1 Susan Sontag, *As Consciousness is Harnessed to Flesh: Diaries, 1964–1980*, ed. David Rieff (London, 2012), p. 334.
2 Ibid., p. 142.
3 Ibid., p. 334.
4 As Larry McCaffery writes, 'the reviews of *Death Kit* almost uniformly indicated that the reviewers had misread Sontag's intentions.' McCaffery also points to the resemblance between *Death Kit* and Borges's short story 'The South': Larry McCaffery, '*Death Kit*: Susan Sontag's Dream Narrative', *Contemporary Literature*, xx/4 (Autumn 1979), p. 487.
5 See *As Consciousness*, p. 60, where Sontag notes Burroughs's shifts from first to third person and back in *Naked Lunch*; Susan Sontag, *Death Kit* (London, 2009), p. 2.
6 *As Consciousness*, p. 61.
7 David Rieff mentions the skull in *Swimming in a Sea of Death: A Son's Memoir* (London, 2008), p. 173.
8 *Death Kit*, p. 4.
9 Ibid., pp. 6–7.
10 Ibid., p. 41.
11 *As Consciousness*, p. 387.
12 *Death Kit*, p. 10.
13 Ibid., p. 11.
14 Ibid., p. 14.
15 Ibid., pp. 166, 111.

16 Ibid., pp. 230 ('Reasons of health'), 250 ('leaking away'), 287 ('Wake up!').

17 *As Consciousness*, pp. 68, 173–4.

18 Sontag mentions Buñuel's interest in filming *Death Kit* in her interview with Evans Chan, 'Against Postmodernism, etc. – A Conversation with Susan Sontag', *Postmodern Culture*, xii/1 (September 2001); Tony Tanner first observed the Didi/Diddy connection, in his discussion of *Death Kit* in *City of Words: American Fiction, 1950–1970* (New York, 1971), pp. 260–72.

19 *As Consciousness*, pp. 65, 143.

20 Ibid., p. 167.

21 Calvin Tomkins, *Duchamp: A Biography* (London, 1997), p. 411, says they met in 1960; in his profile of Jasper Johns, 'The Mind's Eye', *New Yorker* (11 December 2006), p. 85, Tomkins adjusts this to 1959.

22 Leland Poague, ed., *Conversations with Susan Sontag* (Jackson, ms, 1995), p. 186.

23 Carl Rollyson, *Susan Sontag: The Making of an Icon* (New York, 2000), p. 96.

24 There are several boxes of Joseph Cornell material in Sontag's archives at UCLA Library. See Boxes 120–122, Susan Sontag Papers, Charles E. Young Research Library, UCLA Library, Los Angeles.

25 Rachel Cohen recounts the Cornell–Sontag liaison in *A Chance Meeting: Intertwined Lives of American Writers and Artists, 1854–1967* (London, 2004), p. 234.

26 *As Consciousness*, p. 172; *Death Kit*, p. 312.

27 Sontag mentions the inspiration of Hujar's photographs of the Palermo Catacombs in her introduction to Peter Hujar, *Portraits in Life and Death* (New York, 1976).

28 *As Consciousness*, pp. 183–4.

29 Ibid., pp. 190 (Brook), 192 (Grotowski).

30 Ibid., p. 198.

31 Ibid., p. 201.

32 Susan Sontag, 'The Aesthetics of Silence', in *Styles of Radical Will* (London, 2009), p. 3.

33 Ibid., p. 13.

34 Ibid.

35 Ibid., pp. 13, 14, 22.

36 Susan Sontag, '"Thinking Against Oneself": Reflections on Cioran', in *Styles of Radical Will*, p. 79.

37 Ibid., p. 75.

38 Susan Sontag, 'Bergman's *Persona*', in *Styles of Radical Will*, pp. 126, 130, 132.

39 Susan Sontag, 'Godard', in *Styles of Radical Will*, pp. 180, 158.

40 Ibid., p. 158.

41 'Bergman's *Persona*', p. 133.

42 *As Consciousness*, pp. 235, 206.

43 Susan Sontag, 'Trip to Hanoi', in *Styles of Radical Will*, p. 205.

44 Poague, ed., *Conversations*, p. 124.

45 Quoted in Barbara Ching, 'Not Even a New Yorker: Susan Sontag in America', in *The Scandal of Susan Sontag*, ed. Barbara Ching and Jennifer A. Wagner-Lawlor (New York, 2009), p. 60.

46 Susan Sontag, 'Unguided Tour', in *I, Etcetera* (London, 2001), p. 233.

47 'Trip to Hanoi', pp. 270, 271.

48 Ibid., p. 211.

49 Ibid., pp. 214, 220, 225, 226.

50 Ibid., p. 235.

51 Ibid., p. 254.

52 Ibid., p. 273.

53 Ibid., p. 274.

5 In Plato's Cave, 1968–1975

1 Susan Sontag, *Against Interpretation* (London, 2001), p. 11.

2 Susan Sontag, *As Consciousness is Harnessed to Flesh: Diaries, 1964–1980*, ed. David Rieff (London, 2012), p. 254.

3 Susan Sontag, 'The Aesthetics of Silence', in *Styles of Radical Will* (London, 2009), p. 29.

4 Leland Poague, ed., *Conversations with Susan Sontag* (Jackson, MS, 1995), p. 25.

5 Susan Sontag, *Duet for Cannibals: A Screenplay* (London, 1974), p. 62.

6 Ibid., p. 28.

7 Ibid., p. 65.

8 Ibid., p. 105.

9 *As Consciousness*, p. 363.

10 Poague, ed., *Conversations*, p. 26.

11 *As Consciousness*, p. 371.

12 Susan Sontag, 'Trip to Hanoi', in *Styles of Radical Will*, p. 223.

13 *Duet for Cannibals*, p. 20.

14 Susan Sontag, *Reborn: Early Diaries, 1947–1963*, ed. David Rieff (London, 2009), p. 71.

15 *Duet for Cannibals*, p. 79.

16 This account of the 1968 Mexico City talk is recounted in Carl Rollyson, *Susan Sontag: The Making of an Icon* (New York, 2000), p. 129.

17 Susan Sontag, 'Some Thoughts on the Right Way (for Us) to Love the Cuban Revolution', *Ramparts* (April 1969), pp. 6–19.

18 *As Consciousness*, pp. 262 ('passion'), 277 (suicide), 267 ('heroic').

19 Sigrid Nunez, *Sempre Susan* (New York, 2011), p. 54.

20 *As Consciousness*, p. 268.

21 Nunez, *Sempre Susan*, p. 13.

22 Ibid., p. 10.

23 *As Consciousness*, p. 262.

24 'Book Published, Author Walks to Watery Grave', *Kingsport Times* (9 November 1969), p. 5.

25 David Rieff tells us this: *As Consciousness*, p. 108.

26 Susan Sontag, 'Debriefing', in *I, Etcetera* (London, 2001), pp. 51, 52.

27 *As Consciousness*, p. 299.

28 Susan Sontag, *Brother Carl: A Filmscript* (New York, 1974), p. viii.

29 Ibid., p. xv.

30 *As Consciousness*, p. 306.

31 *Brother Carl*, p. xiv.

32 Ibid., p. 41.

33 Susan Sontag, 'Approaching Artaud', in *Under the Sign of Saturn* (London, 2009), p. 35.

34 *As Consciousness*, p. 336.

35 'Debriefing', p. 51.

36 *As Consciousness*, pp. 306, 318.

37 *Brother Carl*, p. xvi.

38 *As Consciousness*, p. 351.

39 Poague, ed., *Conversations*, p. 175.

40 Susan Sontag, 'On Paul Goodman', in *Under the Sign of Saturn*, p. 3.

41 Alice Kaplan, *Dreaming in French: The Paris Years of Jacqueline Bouvier Kennedy, Susan Sontag, and Angela Davis* (Chicago, 2012), p. 255.

42 *As Consciousness*, p. 314.

43 The script of *L'Invitée* is among Sontag's papers at UCLA. See Box 270, Folders 1–7, Susan Sontag Papers, Charles E. Young Research Library, UCLA Library, Los Angeles.

44 Susan Sontag, 'Approaching Artaud', in *Under the Sign of Saturn*, p. 17.

45 *As Consciousness*, p. 360.

46 *As Consciousness*, pp. 27 ('little door'), 361.

47 Ibid., p. 331.

48 Susan Sontag, 'Susan Sontag Tells How it Feels to Make a Movie', *Vogue* (July 1974), pp. 84, 118–19.

49 Ibid.

50 Ibid.

51 *As Consciousness*, p. 384.

52 Ibid., p. 385.

53 Ibid., p. 389.

6 The Kingdom of the Sick, 1975–1988

1 David Rieff, *Swimming in a Sea of Death* (London, 2008), p. 26.

2 Ibid., p. 36.

3 Ibid., pp. 35 ('flattened'), 29 ('leaky panic'), 27 ('daggers'), 28 ('Cancer = death'), 29 ('Everyone's got to die'), 29 ('not ready').

4 Ibid., p. 35.

5 Sigrid Nunez, *Sempre Susan* (New York, 2011), p. 9.

6 Leland Poague, ed., *Conversations with Susan Sontag* (Jackson, MS, 1995), p. 230.

7 Poague, ed., *Conversations*, p. 151.

8 Rieff, *Swimming*, p. 36.

9 Susan Sontag, *As Consciousness is Harnessed to Flesh: Diaries, 1964–1980*, ed. David Rieff (London, 2012), p. 415.

10 Nunez, *Sempre Susan*, p. 33.

11 'He Landed Among Us Like a Missile', interview with Susan Sontag on Joseph Brodsky, in Valentina Polukhina, ed., *Brodsky Through the Eyes of His Contemporaries*, vol. II (Boston, MA, 2008), p. 324.

12 Nunez, *Sempre Susan*, pp. 32, 33.

13 Rieff, *Swimming*, p. 36.

14 *As Consciousness*, p. 426.

15 Nunez, *Sempre Susan*, p. 96.

16 Susan Sontag, 'Under the Sign of Saturn', in *Under the Sign of Saturn* (London, 2009), p. 129.

17 Ibid.

18 Susan Sontag, *On Photography* (London, 2002), pp. 12–13.

19 Poague, ed., *Conversations*, p. 96.

20 *On Photography*, pp. 51, 82.

21 Ibid., p. 81.

22 Ibid., p. 20.

23 Poague, ed., *Conversations*, p. 230.

24 Poague, ed., *Conversations*, p. 197.

25 *As Consciousness*, p. 454.

26 Susan Sontag, *Illness as Metaphor & AIDS and Its Metaphors* (London, 2002), pp. 49, 110.

27 Susan Sontag, *Styles of Radical Will* (London, 2009), p. 203.

28 *Illness*, p. 91.

29 Ibid., p. 98.

30 Ibid., p. 69.

31 Ibid., p. 66.

32 Ibid., p. 56.

33 *As Consciousness*, pp. 434 (Teatro Ateneo), 436 (György Konrád; 'so much beauty'), 445 (vaporetto).

34 Nunez, *Sempre Susan*, p. 113.

35 Poague, ed., *Conversations*, p. 120.

36 Ibid., p. 202.

37 'American Spirits' was originally titled 'The Will and the Way'. See *Partisan Review*, 32 (Summer 1965), pp. 373–96.

38 *As Consciousness*, p. 475. There are several folders related to 'The Japan Project' in the Susan Sontag Papers at UCLA: Box 282, Folders 1–14, Charles E. Young Research Library, UCLA Library, Los Angeles.

39 Poague, ed., *Conversations*, p. 191.

40 Susan Sontag, interview by Arthur Holmberg, *Performing Arts Journal*, IX/1 (1985), p. 29.

41 Poague, ed., *Conversations*, p. 185.

42 Susan Sontag, 'Fascinating Fascism', in *Under the Sign of Saturn*, p. 79.

43 *As Consciousness*, p. 518.

44 Susan Sontag, 'Mind as Passion', in *Under the Sign of Saturn*, p. 204.

45 Poague, ed., *Conversations*, pp. 175 ('liberation'), 197 ('long, complex'), 202 (novella).

46 Joan Acocella mentions the novel 'about a dancer' in 'The Hunger Artist', *New Yorker* (6 March 2000), p. 71; there is a spiral notebook of writing notes, 'Isadora Duncan', in the Susan Sontag Papers at UCLA Library, Box 134, Folder 2.

47 Poague, ed., *Conversations*, p. 202.

48 Acocella, 'The Hunger Artist', p. 71.

49 Callie Angell, *Andy Warhol Screen Tests: The Films of Andy Warhol, Catalogue Raisonné* (New York, 2006), vol. I, pp. 51–3.

50 *As Consciousness*, pp. 420 (a brief note), 498 (Brodsky).

51 Ibid., p. 459.

52 Sontag's version of the Town Hall speech was reprinted with her permission in *The Nation* on 27 February 1982, alongside comments on it from other writers and intellectuals (pp. 231–7).

53 Edmund White, *City Boy: My Life in New York during the 1960s and 1970s* (London, 2010), p. 280.

54 This is how the essay is described in Sohnya Sayres, *Susan Sontag: The Elegiac Modernist* (New York, 1990), p. 43.

55 Notes and drafts of 'Communism and the Intellectuals' are in the Susan Sontag Papers at UCLA Library, Box 275, Folders 1–8.

56 Poague, ed., *Conversations*, p. 208; notes and drafts for 'Sartre's Abdication' are in the Susan Sontag Papers, UCLA Library, Boxes 273–4.

57 Susan Sontag, 'Mr Balanchine', *Vanity Fair* (July 1983), pp. 70–75; Susan Sontag, 'Images of People Past', *Art and Antiques*, 1 (May 1984), pp. 66–77; Susan Sontag, 'Fragments of an Aesthetic of Melancholy', in Vera Lehndorff and Holger Trülzsch, *'Veruschka': Trans-figurations* (London, 1986), pp. 6–12.

58 David Rieff tells us this in *Swimming*, p. 106.

59 Nunez, *Sempre Susan*, pp. 115–16.

60 Susan Sontag, 'The Letter Scene', *New Yorker* (18 August 1986), p. 28.

61 Nunez, *Sempre Susan*, p. 116.

62 Poague, ed., *Conversations*, pp. 256–7.

63 Susan Sontag, *The Way We Live Now* (London, 1991), p. 19.

64 The limited edition of *The Way We Live Now* was published by Karsten Schubert (London, 1990). A different, related trade edition was published by Jonathan Cape (London, 1991).

65 Carl Rollyson and Lisa Paddock, *Susan Sontag: The Making of an Icon* (New York, 2000), p. 257.

66 *Illness*, p. 111.

67 Rieff, *Swimming*, p. 66.

7 Beginning Again, 1988–2000

1 David Van Biema, 'Annie Leibovitz, Face to Face: The Eye of Annie Leibovitz', *Life* (1 April 1994). Quoted in Carl Rollyson and Lisa Paddock, *Susan Sontag: The Making of an Icon* (New York, 2000), p. 280.

2 Annie Leibovitz, introduction to *A Photographer's Life, 1990–2005* (London, 2006), n.p.

3 Leland Poague, ed., *Conversations with Susan Sontag* (Jackson, MS, 1995), p. 264.

4 Leslie Garis, 'Susan Sontag Finds Romance', *New York Times* (2 August 1992), pp. 20–43.

5 Tom Shone, 'Side by Side by Sontag', *Sunday Times Magazine* (2 August 1992), pp. 44–5. Quoted in Liam Kennedy, *Mind as Passion* (Manchester, 1995), p. 119.

6 Susan Sontag, interview in *Paris Review*, 137 (1995), pp. 177–209.

7 Sontag's 'A Parsifal' is in Trevor Fairbrother, *Robert Wilson's Vision* (New York, 1991), pp. 19–27. It is also reprinted, with some changes, in *Antaeus*, LXVII/3 (1991), pp. 180–85.

8 Susan Sontag, *Alice in Bed* (New York, 1993), p. 114.

9 Ibid., p. 117.

10 Ibid., p. 84.

11 Ibid., pp. 30, 117.

12 Interview in *Paris Review*, pp. 177–209.

13 Karla Eoff, 'The Intellectual's Assistant', *Blip Magazine* (2011).

14 Sigrid Nunez, *Sempre Susan* (New York, 2011), p. 23.

15 Harvey Blume, 'The Foreigner', *The Atlantic* (13 April 2000).

16 Susan Sontag, 'A Double Destiny: On Anna Banti's *Artemisia*', in *At the Same Time* (London, 2007), p. 55.

17 Susan Sontag, *The Volcano Lover: A Romance* (New York, 1992), pp. 3–4.

18 Ibid., pp. 19, 131, 132, 351.

19 Garis, 'Susan Sontag Finds Romance', pp. 20–43.

20 *The Volcano Lover*, p. 296.

21 Interview in *Paris Review*, pp. 177–209.

22 *The Volcano Lover*, p. 419.

23 Ibid., pp. 418–19.

24 Susan Sontag, 'Singleness', in *Where the Stress Falls* (London, 2003), pp. 261–2.

25 Susan Sontag, 'About Hodgkin', in *Where the Stress Falls*, pp. 151, 153, 160.

26 Ibid., p. 159.

27 Poague, ed., *Conversations with Susan Sontag*, p. 269.

28 Susan Sontag, 'Waiting for Godot in Sarajevo', in *Where the Stress Falls*, p. 299.

29 Ibid., p. 300.

30 Susan Sontag, 'Trip to Hanoi', in *Styles of Radical Will* (London, 2009), p. 214.

31 Poague, ed., *Conversations with Susan Sontag*, p. 269.

32 'Waiting for Godot in Sarajevo', p. 306.

33 Ibid.

34 Ibid., pp. 311–12.

35 Susan Sontag, '"There" and "Here"', in *Where the Stress Falls*, p. 324.

36 Annie Leibovitz, introduction to *A Photographer's Life*, n.p.

37 Susan Sontag, *In America* (London, 2001), copyright page.

38 Ibid., p. 23.

39 Ibid., p. 27.

40 Ibid., p. 65.

41 Susan Sontag, 'Writing as Reading', in *Where the Stress Falls*, p. 266.

42 *In America*, p. 14.

43 Ibid., p. 123.

44 Ibid., p. 229.

45 Poague, ed., *Conversations with Susan Sontag*, p. 130.

46 Susan Sontag, 'The Conscience of Words', in *At the Same Time*, p. 154.

47 David Rieff, *Swimming in a Sea of Death* (London, 2008), p. 72.

48 'Writing as Reading', p. 265.

49 Ibid.

50 *In America*, p. 374.

51 Ibid., p. 384.

8 The Pain of Others, 2000–2004

1 In their preface to Sontag's *At the Same Time* (London, 2007), p. vii, Paolo Dilonardo and Anne Jump mention the 'novel set in Japan' that Sontag planned to write. Sontag also mentions it in various interviews. In Joan Acocella, 'The Hunger Artist', *New Yorker* (6 March 2000), p. 77, she says the novel will be set in Japan, in the present, 'and it's going to be short. A hundred and twenty pages.' The interviews for the Acocella piece began in 1999. By April and May 2000, Sontag states that the novel will be set in 1930s Japan, with a cast of mainly French characters. See Harvey Blume, *The Atlantic* (13 April 2000), and 'Finding Fact from Fiction', *The Guardian* (27 May 2000).

2 Annie Leibovitz, introduction to *A Photographer's Life, 1990–2005*, n.p.

3 Susan Sontag, 'Danilo Kiš', in *Where the Stress Falls* (London, 2003), p. 96.

4 Susan Sontag, 'Thirty Years Later', in *Where the Stress Falls*, p. 268.

5 Susan Sontag, 'Homage to Halliburton', in *Where the Stress Falls*, p. 255.

6 Susan Sontag, 'A Century of Cinema', in *Where the Stress Falls*, p. 117.

7 For some of the correspondence between Sontag and Leonid Tsypkin's son Mikhail, see the Susan Sontag Papers, UCLA Library, Box 279, Charles E. Young Research Library, UCLA Library, Los Angeles; Susan Sontag, 'Loving Dostoyevsky', in *At the Same Time*, p. 21.

8 Susan Sontag, 'A Few Weeks After', in *At the Same Time*, p. 108.

9 Susan Sontag, '9.11.01', in *At the Same Time*, p. 105.

10 'A Few Weeks After', p. 109.

11 'Finding Fact from Fiction'.

12 'A Few Weeks After', p. 109.

13 Susan Sontag Papers, UCLA Library, Boxes 173–178.

14 Susan Sontag, *Regarding the Pain of Others* (London, 2003), p. 3.

15 Ibid., p. 16.

16 Ibid., p. 18.

17 Ibid., pp. 28, 18, 34.

18 Ibid., p. 40.

19 Ibid., p. 98.

20 Ibid., pp. 102, 113.

21 Dilonardo and Jump, preface to *At the Same Time*, p. vii.

22 Susan Sontag, 'Regarding the Torture of Others', in *At the Same Time*, pp. 133, 131.

23 Ibid., p. 133.

24 Susan Sontag, 'At the Same Time: The Novelist and Moral Reasoning', in *At the Same Time*, p. 222.

25 Wayne Koestenbaum, 'Susan Sontag, Cosmophage', in *The Scandal of Susan Sontag*, ed. Barbara Ching and Jennifer A. Wagner-Lawlor (New York, 2009), p. 236.

26 'At the Same Time: The Novelist and Moral Reasoning', p. 223.

27 David Rieff, *Swimming in a Sea of Death* (London, 2008), pp. 1–11.

28 Ibid., pp. 45, 52–3.

29 Ibid., p. 17.

30 Susan Sontag, *Against Interpretation*, (London, 2001), p. 14.

31 'Finding Fact from Fiction', *The Guardian*.

32 Rieff, *Swimming*, pp. 162–3.

Select Bibliography

Works by Susan Sontag

First edition, followed by edition used in references, where different.

[with/as Philip Rieff], *Freud: The Mind of the Moralist*
    (New York, 1959; New York, 1961)
The Benefactor (New York, 1963; London, 2009)
Against Interpretation (New York, 1966; London, 2001)
Death Kit (New York, 1967; London, 2009)
Trip to Hanoi (New York, 1968)
Styles of Radical Will (New York, 1969; London, 2009)
Duet for Cannibals [film] (Sweden, 1969)
Duet for Cannibals [film script] (London, 1970)
Brother Carl [film] (Sweden, 1971)
Brother Carl [film script] (New York, 1974)
Promised Lands [film] (New York, 1974)
On Photography (New York, 1977; London, 2002)
Illness as Metaphor (New York, 1978; London, 2002)
I, Etcetera (New York, 1978; London, 2001)
Under the Sign of Saturn (New York, 1980; London, 2009)
A Susan Sontag Reader, ed. Sontag (New York, 1982)
Unguided Tour [film] (Italy, 1983)
AIDS and Its Metaphors (New York, 1989; London, 2002)
[with Howard Hodgkin], *The Way We Live Now* (London, 1991)
The Volcano Lover: A Romance (New York, 1992)
Alice in Bed: A Play in Eight Scenes [play] (New York, 1993)
In America (New York, 2000; London, 2001)

Where the Stress Falls: Essays (New York, 2001; London, 2003)

Regarding the Pain of Others (New York, 2003; London, 2003)

At the Same Time: Essays and Speeches, ed. Paolo Dilonardo and Anne Jump
(London, 2007)

Reborn: Early Diaries, 1947–1963, ed. David Rieff (New York, 2008; London,
2009)

As Consciousness is Harnessed to Flesh: Diaries, 1964–1980, ed. David Rieff
(London, 2012)

Other Pieces by Susan Sontag

'Description (of a Description)', *Antaeus*, 53 (1984), pp. 111–14

'The Double Standard of Aging', *Saturday Review* (23 September 1972),
pp. 29–38

'Fragments of an Aesthetic of Melancholy', in Vera Lehndorff and Holger
Trülzsch, *'Veruschka': Trans-figurations* (London, 1986), pp. 6–12

'Francis Bacon: "About Being in Pain"', *Vogue* (March 1975), pp. 136–7

'Images of People Past', *Art and Antiques*, 1 (May 1984), pp. 66–77

'Introduction' to Peter Hujar, *Portraits in Life and Death* (New York, 1976)

'Lady from the Sea', *Theater*, xxix/1 (1999), pp. 93–115

'The Letter Scene', *New Yorker* (18 August 1986), pp. 24–32

'A Letter from Sweden', *Ramparts* (July 1969), pp. 23–38

'Mr Balanchine', *Vanity Fair* (July 1983), pp. 70–75

[with David Rieff], 'Notes on Optimism', *Vogue* (January 1975), pp. 100,
148, 154

'A Parsifal', in Trevor Fairbrother, *Robert Wilson's Vision* (New York, 1991),
pp. 19–27. Also published, with changes, in *Antaeus*, lxvii/3 (1991),
pp. 180–85

'Pilgrimage', *New Yorker* (21 December 1987), pp. 38–54

'Posters: Advertisement, Art, Political Artefact, Commodity', in
The Art of Revolution, ed. Dugald Stermer (New York, 1970),
pp. vii–xxiii

'Preface', in *María Irene Fornés: Plays* (New York, 1986), pp. 7–10

[as 'Calvin Koff'], 'Some Notes on Antonioni and Others'. Reprinted
with an introduction by Colin Burnett, *Post Script*, xxvi/2 (2007),
pp. 137–42

'Some Thoughts on the Right Way (for Us) to Love the Cuban Revolution',
  Ramparts (April 1969), pp. 6–19
'Susan Sontag Tells How it Feels to Make a Movie', *Vogue* (July 1974),
  pp. 84, 118–19
'The Third World of Women', *Partisan Review* (Spring 1973), pp. 180–206
'The View from the Ark', in Richard Misrach, *Violent Legacies: Three Cantos*
  (New York, 1992), pp. 9–12

Interviews

Acocella, Joan, 'The Hunger Artist', *New Yorker* (6 March 2000), pp. 68–77
Blume, Harvey, 'The Foreigner', *The Atlantic* (13 April 2000), at
  www.theatlantic.com
Bockris, Victor, 'Sontag + Hell', Victor Bockris, Richard Hell, *Interview*
  (April 1978), pp. 28–30
—, 'Susan Sontag: The Dark Lady of Pop Philosophy', *High Times*
  (March 1978), pp. 20–37
Brennan, Paul, 'Sontag in Greenwich Village: An Interview', *London
  Magazine* (April–May 1979), pp. 93–103
Brockes, Emma, 'My Time With Susan', interview with Annie Leibovitz,
  Guardian (7 October 2006), pp. 18–35
Chan, Evans, 'Against Postmodernism, etcetera – A Conversation with
  Susan Sontag', *Postmodern Culture*, xii/1 (September 2001),
  www.iath.virginia.edu/pmc
'Finding Fact from Fiction', *The Guardian* (27 May 2000),
  www.guardian.co.uk
Garis, Leslie, 'Susan Sontag Finds Romance', *New York Times* (2 August
  1992), pp. 20–43
Heller, Zoë, 'The Life of a Head Girl', *Independent on Sunday: Review*
  (20 September 1992), pp. 10–12
Hirsch, Edward, 'Susan Sontag: The Art of Fiction', *Paris Review*, 137
  (1995), pp. 177–209
Holmberg, Arthur, 'Susan Sontag', *Performing Arts Journal*, ix/1 (1985),
  pp. 28–30
Low, Lisa, 'Interview with Susan Sontag', *Cross Currents*, 8 (1989),
  pp. 185–93

Munk, Erika, 'Only the Possible: An Interview with Susan Sontag',
  Theater, 24 (1993), pp. 31–6
Poague, Leland, ed., *Conversations with Susan Sontag* (Jackson, MS, 1995)
Polukhina, Valentina, 'He Landed Among Us Like a Missile', in *Brodsky
  Through the Eyes of His Contemporaries*, ed. Polukhina, vol. II
  (Boston, MA, 2008), pp. 323–32

Archives and Bibliography

Poague, Leland, and Kathy A. Parsons, *Susan Sontag: An Annotated
  Bibliography, 1948–1992* (New York, 2000)
The Susan Sontag Papers *c*. 1939–2004, Department of Special
  Collections, Charles E. Young Library, University of California
  at Los Angeles Library

Biography, Criticism, Memoir

Angell, Callie, *Andy Warhol Screen Tests: The Films of Andy Warhol Catalogue
  Raisonné*, vol. I (New York, 2006)
Athill, Diana, 'Afterword', in Alfred Chester, *The Exquisite Corpse* (Boston,
  MA, 2003). Adapted from Diana Athill, *Stet: A Memoir* (London,
  2000)
Berger, John, 'Photography: God of the Instant', *Seven Days* (7 April 1978),
  pp. 28–30
Boyd Maunsell, Jerome, 'A Little Door', TLS (1 June 2012), p. 25
—, 'The Writer's Diary as Device: The Making of Susan Sontag in *Reborn:
  Early Diaries, 1947–1963*', *Journal of Modern Literature*, XXXV/1 (2011),
  pp. 1–20
Campbell, James, *Paris Interzone: Richard Wright, Lolita, Boris Vian and
  Others on the Left Bank, 1946–60* (London, 1994)
Castle, Terry, 'Desperately Seeking Susan', *London Review of Books*
  (17 March 2005), pp. 17–20
Ching, Barbara, and Jennifer A. Wagner-Lawlor, 'High Regard: Words and
  Pictures in Tribute to Susan Sontag', *American Quarterly*, LIX/1 (2007),
  pp. 157–64

—, eds, *The Scandal of Susan Sontag* (New York, 2009)

Cohen, Rachel, *A Chance Meeting: Intertwined Lives of American Writers and Artists, 1854–1967* (London, 2004)

Eoff, Karla, 'The Intellectual's Assistant', *Blip Magazine* (Winter 2011), www.blipmagazine.net

Field, Edward, *The Man Who Would Marry Susan Sontag* (Madison, WI, 2005)

—, 'The Mystery of Alfred Chester', *Boston Review*, XVIII/2 (1993)

Hardwick, Elizabeth, 'Knowing Sontag', *Vogue* (June 1978), pp. 184–5

Indiana, Gary, 'Susan Sontag's *Unguided Tour*', *Artforum*, XXII/3 (November 1983), pp. 66–8

Kaplan, Alice, *Dreaming in French: The Paris Years of Jacqueline Bouvier Kennedy, Susan Sontag, and Angela Davis* (Chicago, IL, 2012)

Kennedy, Liam, 'Precocious Archaeology: Susan Sontag and the Criticism of Culture', *Journal of American Studies*, XXIV/1 (1990), pp. 23–39

—, *Susan Sontag: Mind as Passion* (Manchester, 1995)

Koch, Stephen, 'On Susan Sontag', *TriQuarterly*, 7 (1966), pp. 152–60

Leibovitz, Annie, *A Photographer's Life, 1990–2005* (London, 2006)

—, *Women* (New York, 1999)

Lopate, Phillip, *Notes on Sontag* (Princeton, NJ, 2009)

McCaffery, Larry, '*Death Kit*: Susan Sontag's Dream Narrative', *Contemporary Literature*, XX/4 (1979), pp. 484–99

McEwan, Ian, 'Kamera Obskura', *New Statesman* (29 September 1978), pp. 410–11

McRobbie, Angela, 'The Modernist Style of Susan Sontag', *Feminist Review*, 38 (1991), pp. 1–19

Mapplethorpe, Robert, *Certain People: A Book of Portraits* (Pasadena, CA, 1985)

Meyer, Sara, 'Susan Sontag's "Archaeology of Longings"', *Texas Studies in Literature and Language*, XLIX/1 (Spring 2007), pp. 45–63

Nelson, Cary, 'Soliciting Self-Knowledge: The Rhetoric of Susan Sontag's Criticism', *Critical Inquiry*, VI/4 (1980), pp. 707–26

Nunez, Sigrid, *Sempre Susan: A Memoir of Susan Sontag* (New York, 2011)

Ozick, Cynthia, 'Alfred Chester's Wig', *New Yorker* (30 March 1992), pp. 79–98

—, *The Din in the Head: Essays* (New York, 2006)

—, *Foreign Bodies* (New York, 2011)

Phillips, William, 'Radical Styles', *Partisan Review*, 36 (Summer 1969), pp. 388–400

Rieff, David, *Swimming in a Sea of Death: A Son's Memoir* (London, 2008)

Rollyson, Carl, and Lisa Paddock, *Reading Susan Sontag: A Critical Introduction to Her Work* (Chicago, IL, 2001)

—, *Susan Sontag: The Making of an Icon* (New York, 2000)

Sayres, Sohnya, 'Susan Sontag and the Practice of Modernism', *American Literary History*, 1/3 (1989), pp. 593–611

—, *Susan Sontag: The Elegiac Modernist* (New York, 1990)

Seligman, Craig, *Sontag and Kael: Opposites Attract Me* (New York, 2005)

Shipman, Dru, 'Sontag on Photography', *Afterimage*, 11/7 (January 1975), pp. 4–12

Solotaroff, Theodore, 'Death in Life', *Commentary* (November 1967), pp. 87–9

Tanner, Tony, *City of Words: American Fiction, 1950–1970* (New York, 1971)

Tomkins, Calvin, *Duchamp: A Biography* (London, 1997)

—, 'The Mind's Eye: The Merciless Originality of Jasper Johns', *New Yorker* (11 December 2006), pp. 76–85

Toynbee, Philip, 'Critique of Freud', *Encounter* (April 1960), pp. 73–6

Vidal, Gore, 'The Writer as Cannibal', *Chicago Tribune Book World* (10 September 1967), pp. 5, 34

White, Edmund, *City Boy: My Life in New York During the 1960s and 1970s* (London, 2010)

Wood, Michael, 'Susan Sontag and the American Will', *Raritan*, XXI/1 (2001), pp. 141–7

Zwerling, Harriet Sohmers, 'A Memoir of Alfred Chester', *Raritan*, XXII/3 (1993). Reprinted in Harriet Sohmers Zwerling, *Notes of a Nude Model* (New York, 2003), and as 'Afterword', in Alfred Chester, *Jamie is My Heart's Desire* (Boston, MA, 2007)

—, 'Memories of Sontag: From an Ex-Pat's Diary', *The Brooklyn Rail* (2006), www.brooklynrail.org

Acknowledgements

I would like to thank, for various reasons, Rosemary Ashton, Clare Brant, James Burrell, Edward Clarke, Andy Cooke, Mark Currie, Jane Darcy, Santanu Das, Brian Dillon, Rozalind Dineen, Lindsay Duguid, James Eve, Lara Feigel, Mark Ford, Dan Fox, Ronnie Graham, Sara Haslam, Oliver Herford, Jennifer Higgie, Ross Hornblower, Philip Horne, Ann Kaplan, Edith Kurzweil, Katie Law, Hermione Lee, Toby Lichtig, Angela McRobbie, Brenda Maddox, Nathaniel Mellors, David Miller, John Mullan, Anne Hilde Neset, Leonee Ormond, Robert Patrick, Patricia Phillippy, Ariel Pintor, Huw Price, James Roberts, Max Saunders, David Sexton, Hugo Shuttleworth, William Skidelsky, Anna Snaith, Anna Vaux, Jonathan Walton, Alison Wood, Jessica Woollard and Rob Young. This book also could not have been written without all the support of my family.

I'm also extremely grateful to Michael Leaman, Martha Jay and Harry Gilonis at Reaktion for their work on this book. For help with the illustrations, many thanks to James Campbell, Terry Castle (for advice on Sontag's High School Yearbook photograph), Barbara Ching, Edward Field, Jim Gossage, Peggy Kaplan, Stephen Koch, Christina Pareigis, Amy DiPasquale, Ethan and Tanaquil Taubes, Jennifer Wagner Lawlor and Harriet Sohmers Zwerling.

Photo Acknowledgements

The author and publishers wish to express their thanks to the following sources of illustrative material and/or permission to reproduce it.

Photo © Bob Adelman/CORBIS: p. 69; Arizona Historical Society, Tucson: p. 14; photo © Sophie Bassouls/Sygma/CORBIS: p. 140; photos © Bettmann/CORBIS: pp. 113, 123; photo Werner W. Christmann © Bettmann/CORBIS: p. 24; courtesy Edward Field: p. 74; courtesy Edward Field/Harriet Sohmers Zwerling: pp. 40, 43; photo James D. Gossage: p. 49; from William Hamilton, *Campi Phlegraei: Observations on the Volcanos of the Two Sicilies . . .* vol. III (Naples, 1779): p. 152; © 1987 The Peter Hujar Archive LCC – reproduced courtesy Pace/MacGill Gallery, New York, and Fraenkel Gallery, San Francisco: p. 72; © The Joseph and Robert Cornell Memorial Foundation/VAGA, NY/DACS, London 2013: p. 84; Peggy Jarrell Kaplan: p. 136; Stephen Koch/Peter Hujar estate: p. 72; courtesy Edith Kurzweil: p. 18; © Magnum Photos, courtesy Fondation Henri Cartier-Bresson: p. 6; Mapplethorpe estate: p. 147; © The New York Public Library for the Performing Arts, Billy Rose Theatre Division: p. 49; from *Partisan Review*, vol. XV, no. 12 (December 1948): p. 18; private collection: p. 84; private collection/Index/The Bridgeman Art Library: p. 177; private collection/The Stapleton Collection/The Bridgeman Art Library: p. 152; private collection/Ken Walsh/The Bridgeman Art Library: p. 155; photo Rex Features/Everett Collection: p. 71; photo Rex Features/Roger-Viollet: p. 110; reproduced with the kind permission of Ethan and Tanaquil Taubes: p. 29; University of Pennsylvania Archives, Philadelphia: p. 27; © 2014 The Andy Warhol Museum, Pittsburgh, PA, a museum of Carnegie Institute – all rights reserved: p. 68; from Alfred Whitman, *The Print-collector's Handbook*

(London, 1901): p. 155; Zentrum für Literatur- und Kulturforschung, Berlin: p. 29.